Mike,

Have fun cooking

All the best!

JOE

KNOWS

FISH

TAKING THE INTIMIDATION
OUT OF COOKING SEAFOOD

JOE GURRERA

owner of

FINE FOODS

with Rebecca Miller Ffrench

CITARELLA PRESS

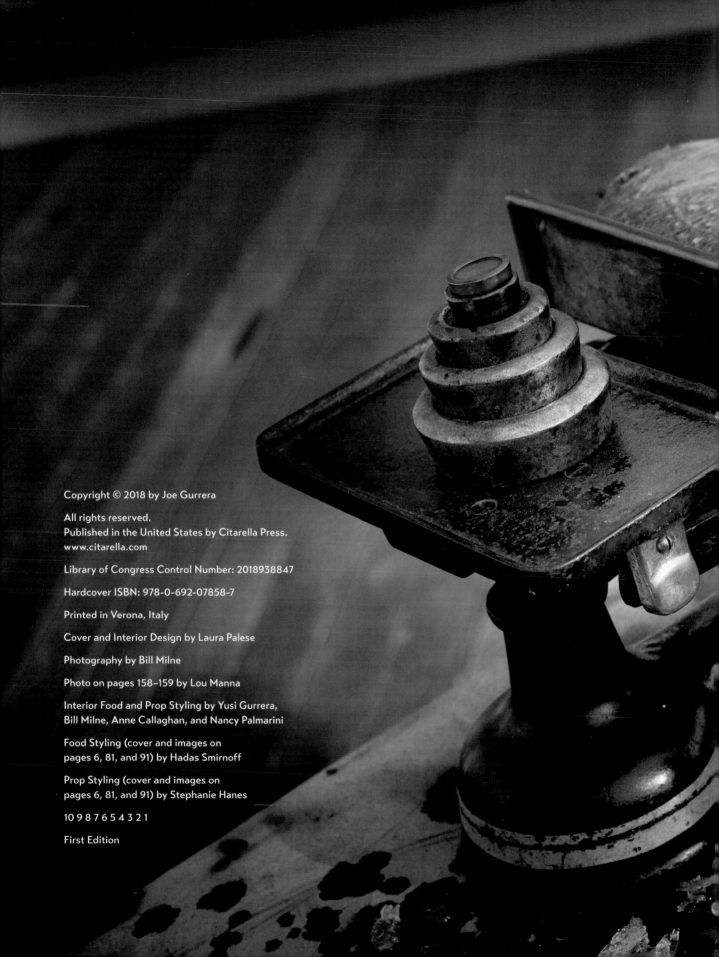

Library of Congress Control Number: 2018938847

Hardcover ISBN: 978-0-692-07858-7

Printed in Verona, Italy

Cover and Interior Design by Laura Palese

Photography by Bill Milne

Photo on pages 158–159 by Lou Manna

Interior Food and Prop Styling by Yusi Gurrera,
Bill Milne, Anne Callaghan, and Nancy Palmarini

Food Styling (cover and images on
pages 6, 81, and 91) by Hadas Smirnoff

Prop Styling (cover and images on
pages 6, 81, and 91) by Stephanie Hanes

10 9 8 7 6 5 4 3 2 1

First Edition

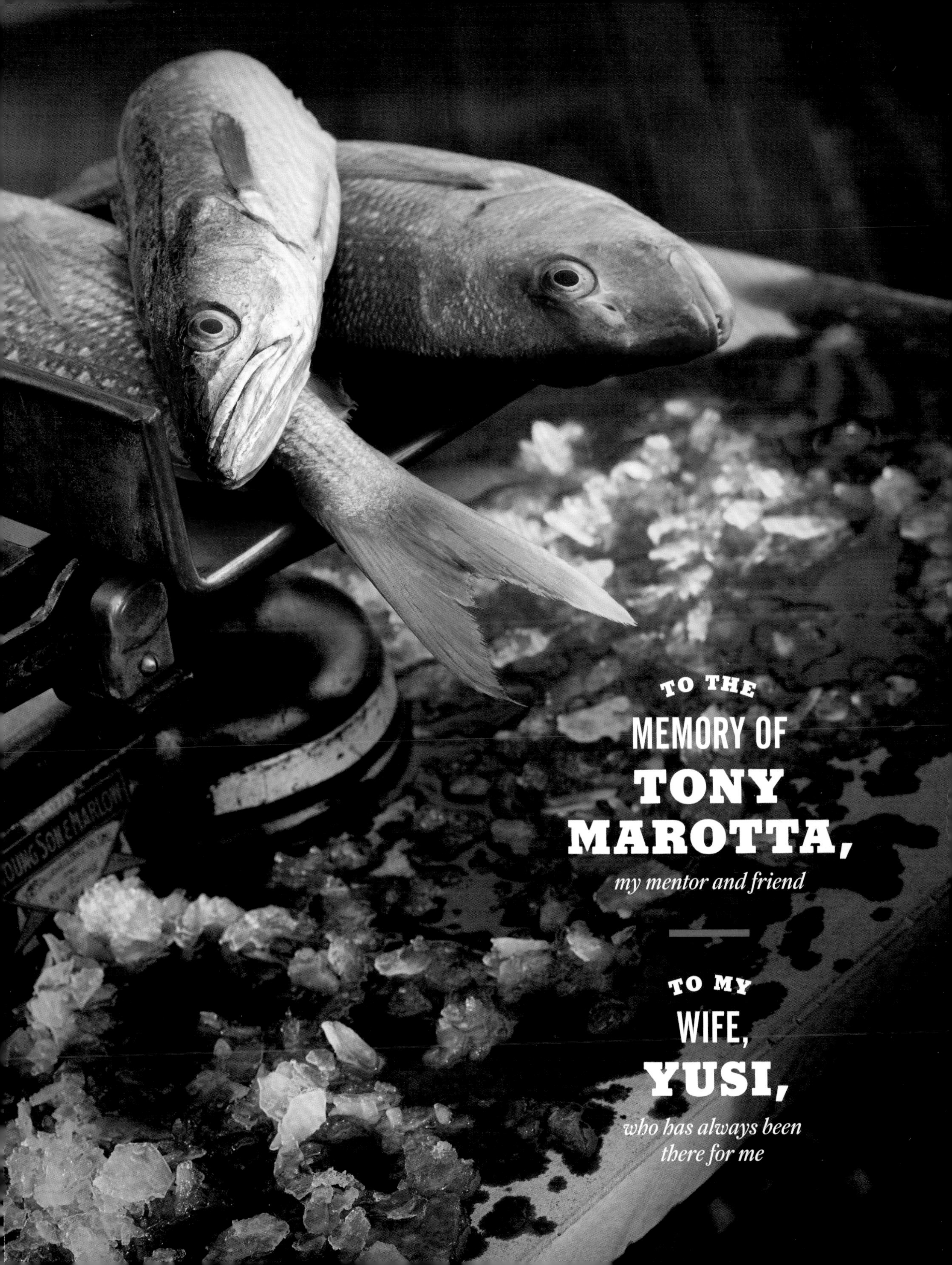

TO THE
MEMORY OF
TONY
MAROTTA,
my mentor and friend

———

TO MY
WIFE,
YUSI,
who has always been
there for me

CONTENTS

INTRODUCTION

Because I want to take the intimidation out of cooking seafood.

For years, people have been telling me they're afraid to cook fish. And I get it, America is a burger country. If you grew up eating fish, you're lucky. Most people didn't and are put off by it. They just don't know what to do with it—they don't know how to buy, handle, or cook it. And if they do buy fish or seafood, they're worried they're going to ruin it. I promise, if you follow what I'm saying, you'll taste fish at its very best. You'll wonder what you ever feared.

And why me? Who am I to tell you how to cook fish? Well, my name is Joe Gurrera, and I own one of New York's original and most-respected seafood shops—Citarella. Some even call me Mr. Citarella. But that's not what makes me qualified. I don't believe a title gets you respect—you've got to earn it.

So I've spent years, nearly my entire life, learning the subtle differences between the flavors and textures of dozens of varieties of seafood. My father took me, a first-generation Italian kid, to the Fulton Fish Market—a gritty, outdoor space that was right under the Brooklyn Bridge—for the first time when I was ten (the market has since moved to Hunts Point in the Bronx). I started going to the market on my own when I was seventeen. Then at twenty-four I was delivering fish across the country—and by the time I was twenty-eight, I owned my own shop. I'm living the American dream.

I've also worked with and learned from some of the best guys in the business. My big break came in the late '70s when Wolfgang Puck, then a young chef in Los Angeles at Ma Maison, called me. He had heard from a fellow chef at the Doral hotel here in New York that a

Clockwise from upper-left: Citarella
present day; Citarella 1954; Joe
(R) and Anthony Bencivenga,
long-time co-worker and buddy
(L); Citarella truck 1920s

twenty-four-year-old guy (me) was supplying him with some great fish. Encouraged by my mentor, Tony Marotta, I hopped on a $99 flight to California to go meet Wolfgang.

This was a big deal for a Brooklyn kid like me. Rebellious and unknowing, I showed up at noon to talk to a chef during lunch service, one of the busiest times of day. Nevertheless, Wolfgang still welcomed me. And out of that meeting came a string of clients on the West Coast—including Michael's and Valentino in Santa Monica—and that's what got me started.

I would personally source and hand-pack the orders with ice packs for these restaurants, then I'd take the seafood cartons to cargo at JFK, go around the front of the terminal and hop on the same plane, get off in LA six hours later, rent a van, get the cargo, deliver it to all the restaurants, and fly back to New York on the red-eye.

It wasn't sexy, and it wasn't easy. My days were long, but I found my passion. I do admit though, LA in the '80s was a scene! I was supplying some of the hottest restaurants in town, including Trumps (no relation to Donald) on Melrose. It was *the* place to be, and you knew big deals were being made there. Jimmy's, in Beverly Hills, with its Rodeo Drive clientele, was crowded with celebrities and socialites.

During that same time back in New York—1983 to be exact—I made a decision that would change my life. I'd been working at our family's seafood shop in Greenwich Village but was itching for something of my own. I heard that a very small, traditional seafood market, the old-fashioned kind with sawdust on the floor, called Citarella was for sale on Manhattan's Upper West Side. The market, which had been around since 1912, had a good reputation and a loyal neighborhood following. I had earned enough money from my West Coast endeavor to buy it. After only one year under my ownership, Citarella was gaining recognition and was voted #1 by Zagat Survey. Over the years, I've grown that little seafood shop into seven full-service gourmet markets in New York City, the Hamptons, and Connecticut.

One day Abe Haymes, a wholesaler at the Fulton Fish Market, told me he was splitting with his associate. I jumped at the opportunity and we became partners. About a year later, Abe sold his portion of the business to me. I applied myself and built that single-stall supplier, Lockwood & Winant, into the largest square-footage wholesale seafood company in the Fulton Fish Market and in 2007, opened Meat Without Feet, a seafood hospitality purveyor.

My father took me, a FIRST-GENERATION ITALIAN KID, to the Fulton Fish Market—a gritty, outdoor space that was right under the Brooklyn Bridge—for the first time when I was ten.

MEAT WITHOUT FEET

Lockwood & Winant

And while my scope has expanded greatly from those beginnings, when I'd work the fish market at night and the store by day, I'm still a hands-on guy. I make my rounds daily from our stores up to the Bronx, where the Fulton Fish Market and Citarella kitchens and warehouse are located.

Together with my buyers and salesmen, we're still sourcing fresh fish every day and maintaining long-standing relationships we have with our trusted fishermen. We even go abroad to places like Iceland, Norway, Greece, New Zealand, Australia, South Africa, and South America to seek out suppliers.

Even though I'm involved in every aspect of the businesses, I pride myself on my team: salesmen, chefs, fishmongers, butchers, produce guys, and bakers—all of them experts in their areas of specialty. With almost 1,000 employees, together we've grown the business to serve almost 5 million customers a year. But it's not numbers that drive me. It's my passion for excellence.

You'll see New York's most well-respected chefs coming to our stores to buy seafood if they're running low at their restaurants—and also when they're cooking for themselves at home. This speaks to the quality of our fish more than I ever could. We are very particular about how our fish are handled. We keep everything meticulously clean, and the fish are treated with tender-loving care. We don't package our fish in Styrofoam containers and plastic wrap like you find in supermarkets. We keep our fish on shaved ice, and we don't freeze fresh fish. Ever. I'm obsessed with freshness.

We focus on quality in all areas, not just seafood. We use the freshest ingredients—like sea salt and high-grade extra-virgin olive oil. Using quality staples like these can make a big difference in your everyday cooking. If you don't already, start using them and you'll notice the improvement in flavor.

Seafood has been my life and I want to share what I know with you. I cook it and eat it five to seven days a week by choice. While I'm not a professionally trained chef, I've spent hundreds of hours in the kitchen preparing seafood and developing techniques and recipes. I want to show you how to grill the best branzino, stuff and bake a tender calamari, and broil the perfect red snapper. My goal is to show you techniques that are so simple you'll feel at ease cooking these dishes too.

A hard-shell crab shedding its shell to become a soft-shell crab.

MY PROMISE TO YOU

I want you to view this book as an introduction to preparing seafood and me as your personal guide, teaching you how to cook it correctly so you can appreciate the flavors of different types of fish.

Everything you eat is about flavor or texture. I'm going to give you an example: when people eat beef they order filet mignon for texture and rib or shell steak for flavor. The same is true for seafood: shrimp is about texture and salmon is about flavor.

I think all fish are delicious, but it's up to you to decide for yourself which fish *you* like best. Once you're familiar with the variety of tastes and preparations, then you can get creative. But you may not even want to—I still prefer my fish simply prepared. While most of my recipes don't include sauces, I've included a few classic ones at the end of the book. I've also shared recipes for my favorite sides, which are equally easy to prepare. They provide color, interest, and complementary flavors to the fish.

When I hear someone tell me they don't like cod, or fluke, or halibut, **I SAY WRONG!**

You know why? Because maybe it was **NOT FRESH**, or maybe it was **OVERCOOKED**. I'm going to show you how to cook it the **RIGHT WAY**.

My cooking methods work, I promise. I walk you through six different techniques I use for preparing fish and seafood, from grilling, baking, and broiling, to sautéing, poaching, and frying. I also share a few favorite pasta recipes and show you how to serve raw and chilled seafood. Because this is a book for beginners, I include the exact cuts or preparations you should request from your fishmonger. Let him or her do the work. By the time you finish this book, you should be comfortable with preparing (and eating!) seafood.

Also note that I'm a born-and-bred New Yorker. I'm going to talk to you straight like I do my family and friends. I won't hesitate to tell you NOT to pick up your cell phone when you're cooking fish. You do it and your fish is ruined because every minute counts when cooking seafood! Trust me. Beyond my sometimes bold tone is knowledge and a true love of fish and cooking—and a passion for passing it along to my customers, and now you.

HOW I COOK

When you cook fresh fish, it doesn't take much to make it delicious. The key: freshness and timing. No matter what you're cooking, a delicious end result can come only from paying attention.

You're going to find many recipes in this book using only four basic ingredients: fish, salt, pepper, and olive oil. I've kept the seasonings simple on purpose because nature has given us original flavors, and I don't want to mask them. Sometimes a recipe will require more, sometimes less. I'll give you the easiest possible methods for making fish and seafood taste its absolute best.

Then, after you've eaten properly cooked seafood, you'll be able to determine what each one tastes like. If you really concentrate on what you're eating, you'll be able to detect the subtle and not so subtle flavor and texture differences—mild, sweet, delicate, meaty, fatty, and robust—between types of fish. I often hear people say they don't like fish. But which one don't they like? Fish is actually quite fascinating in that it has such a wide variety within its class, more so than most any other animal. Before someone gives up on seafood, I encourage them to sample a few different kinds to see if there's one that strikes their palate.

SALT
TO TASTE

I ALWAYS USE SEA SALT, which is naturally low in sodium. It is made up of crystals that stick to food, as opposed to the fine texture of table salt, which dissolves quickly and is actually much saltier tasting than sea salt.

I find some people shy away from using salt. Unless your doctor advises against it, don't be afraid to use it.

Ask most any chef what makes restaurant food taste so good, and they're likely to say, "proper seasoning." Keep in mind that some seafood has a naturally salty flavor, so be sure to start out slowly, but don't hesitate to keep going. Throughout the book I say "season to taste" and encourage you to taste as you go. You want the salt to heighten the taste of the food, but it should never taste salty.

I almost always use my fingers, and not teaspoon measures, when seasoning with salt. You can pinch sea salt better than finer salt, which is another reason I like it. For example, two to three good pinches of salt should be enough for one pan of sautéed spinach. Hold your fingers 8 to 12 inches above the food you're seasoning, and release the salt as you sprinkle it over your food.

There are also instances where I use specialty salts like French grey salt or Hawaiian salt, but these are not a must. I believe learning to season is one of the first steps to cooking delicious food.

FEMALE

MALE

THE LAST LEGS OF A
MALE LOBSTER
ARE **THICK,**

AS OPPOSED TO A
FEMALE'S,
WHICH ARE MORE
FEATHERY

TIMING IS A MUST

So what matters most when cooking fish? Timing! You will hear me say again, and again, and again: TIMING IS EVERYTHING. If you cook fish quickly over a medium-high heat, you're almost always guaranteed a perfectly moist, fragrant, appetizing outcome.

If you're going to stick with me through this book, I want you to promise to take timing seriously and that you'll never rush. Don't mess up a good piece of fish by not paying attention.

Buy a timer. Hang a clock on the wall. You can use the timer on your phone, but don't you dare start reading text messages—USE ONLY THE TIMER.

Once you take a bite of a tender shrimp or a sautéed striped bass fillet with an irresistibly crispy skin, you'll understand how careful timing is the secret to perfectly cooked seafood.

CLEAN EATING

I have a simple and direct approach to life that I apply to my cooking. Because I eat simply—rarely any sauces or sugar—I eat clean by default. Eating simply is a naturally healthy way to live, and the nourishing properties of fish are just an added bonus in my opinion. I'd like to say you'll live five years longer from eating this way, but I can't guarantee it. I eat fish because I love the taste.

One ingredient you'll notice I use often is olive oil. Maybe it's my Sicilian roots (all four of my grandparents were from Sicily), but it's also good for you and gives a perfect result every time.

If you're not already familiar with different types of olive oil, spend some time getting to know them. There are many varieties, and the flavors can range from sweet to sharp and pungent. I recommend opting for one that's full flavored but not too strong when cooking fish.

I don't cook in butter because the flavor can overpower the fish. When you cook fish correctly, it becomes buttery rich itself. I'm not saying you can't use butter—there's definitely a place for it—but you certainly don't need it for the purposes of this book. By allowing the flavor to come through, you'll stretch your palate if you're not already familiar with fish. This way, you'll learn what types of fish you love the most. It'll educate you. Take notes. Cook two types of fish side by side. Do a little taste test to really help you decipher differences.

WANT TO
know the
SECRET
TO
COOKING
FISH?

—

Tick-tock. **Timing!**
Trust me on this.
Never overcook fish.
That's it.
It's that easy.

FISH & THE
FOOD REVOLUTION

IN THE '70S, WHEN I STARTED IN THE SEAFOOD BUSINESS, there was a shift toward eating healthier, fresher foods. Chefs like Alice Waters, Wolfgang Puck, Jonathan Waxman, and Piero Selvaggio were choosing ingredients for their natural flavors—they wanted their fish as fresh as the produce they were getting from local farms. I got it. The fresher the better. It was in those early days when I established what would be my business practices for life: quality, freshness, and value. And that's why I got the chance to supply these chefs. I could get what they wanted. I wanted it too.

I worked with fishermen to figure out how I could get the best product. Some of it depended on advances in packaging and transportation, which resulted in the better handling of fish and therefore a higher quality.

Today, because of farmed fish and fish-population management, all types of fresh fish are available on a greater scale. So while you can get salmon year-round now, not every fresh fish is available daily. It is still a commodity, and prices can shift depending on supply and demand. You should see our wholesale offices. It's like a trading floor in the early mornings. "Hey Joe, how much for the striped bass?" "There's a glut of crabs...the price is dropping." "I'll try to get $50 a bushel, not sure I can."

Sustainability is top of mind these days. People want to eat fish knowing that what they're eating is not harming the ecosystem. Sustainable fishing is maintaining the harvesting rate so the fish population does not decline over time. We sell seafood that is either wild-caught or farmed in sustainable ways. We also follow standards set by the National Oceanic and Atmospheric Administration (NOAA), which works to manage fish populations through quotas and permits. We take these standards seriously and work only with fishermen who follow these legal regulations. Along with airlines, fishing is one of the top ten most-regulated industries in the United States.

WHERE TO START

BUY

THE BEST-

QUALITY

fish you can.

Getting the best-quality fish begins with a great seafood shop.

Look for a place that offers a wide selection and has lots of turnover. Finding high-grade seafood is half the meal prep, and can be MORE intimidating than cooking the fish itself. If you develop a relationship with a reputable fishmonger, you'll get to know and trust his or her selection. (I happen to know one that can overnight fish anywhere in the US!)

USE YOUR SENSES

Using your eyes and nose is the best way to familiarize yourself with raw seafood.

Spend some time comparing fish, taking note of what looks good and what doesn't. The fish should be bright and shiny, and its spots, lines, and markings should be sharp and crisp. The skin should glisten and not be dull. A fresh fish should be firm, not mushy.

Another thing you should take into account when buying fish is its odor. Shop with your nose.

Do you know why Citarella stores never smell fishy? Because fresh fish doesn't smell—and our fish is always fresh. When you walk out on a dock and get a whiff of a strong fishy scent, you're smelling the wood that's holding those odors, not the fish. We revolutionized the traditional seafood shop setup just for that reason. There is no wood or sawdust to absorb smells. In our markets we use materials like stainless steel and granite.

The more you see and smell, the better judge you'll become. Think of it like choosing produce in the store. You can most likely tell if a banana's ripe, right? Is it bright and yellow or black, mushy, and overripe? It's the same with fish. Familiarize yourself with fish and you'll learn the signs of freshness.

TRUST YOUR SOURCE

People are always asking me how they'll know if fish is fresh. I'll tell you, so much of it is about experience. Because I've handled thousands of pounds of fish, I know the difference immediately—it's become second nature to me. Until you have some experience, you need to rely on the person you're buying fish and seafood from. You need to trust them.

And how does a fishmonger gain that trust? Word of mouth is generally pretty reliable. What's the fishmonger's reputation? Talk with the person behind the counter. Spend some time there asking about the fish. When did he get it? Where was it caught?

You'll hear people say that stores have fresh fish on Mondays, but you really don't know what they're putting out. They could have gotten it the week prior. The day of the week doesn't matter if you've built that trust.

ASK YOUR FISHMONGER FOR HELP

I could ask you to fillet every fish you're cooking, but that could get intimidating. Instead, rely on your fishmonger to do the work. If you're buying a whole fish, ask them to clean it for you, which entails gutting it and removing the scales. You can also ask them to fillet it, skin it, and maybe even pull the pin bones—those tiny little bones in the meat.

You can even ask your fishmonger to shuck oysters and clams for you. (There's always the option of flying me out to wherever you live, and I'd be happy to show you how to do it in person!) But seriously, our fish guys at Citarella hand-cut fish and prepare seafood every day that gets sent overnight all across the country (check out our selection at citarella.com), so no matter where you live in the US you can get fresh seafood. Call and we'd be happy to answer any questions about fish. Throughout the book, look for the "Ask Your Fishmonger" icon, where you'll find exactly what cut or preparation you'll need for a specific recipe when special instructions are required.

At Lockwood & Winant with my son Anthony

Like many things, **YOU GET WHAT YOU PAY FOR.** Fish falls into that category. It's better to eat **GOOD-QUALITY** fish less often than substandard fish every day.

COOKING

WITH JOE

—

THE
RULES

I hate rules. Period. *But there are certain rules that should
be respected. Take the National Oceanic and Atmospheric Administration
(NOAA). We follow their quotas to the letter.*

*And then there are my own rules for cooking fish. I absolutely
abide by these. When you cook with me, consider these the
Seven Commandments for Successfully Cooking Seafood.*

1 Use the **freshest ingredients**. Always.

2 Depend on a **timer**, not a thermometer, when cooking fish.

3 **Pay attention**. Don't pick up your phone or leave the room.

4 Always **rinse and pat fish dry**.

5 **Preheat your pan or grill**, getting it nice and hot before fish touches it.

6 When cooking fish, **flip it only once**. Don't ever do it twice.

7 **Cook and serve fish immediately**— but, despite what people think, leftovers are fine the next day.

IT'S ALL ABOUT
RELATIONSHIPS:
SEEKING OUT THE BEST SUPPLIERS

—

JUST LIKE I TOLD YOU TO GET TO KNOW YOUR FISHMONGER, I've done the same with my purveyors through my wholesale business Lockwood & Winant. To me, it is important to understand how the seafood we're buying is handled during all stages, from the water to the docks to the market. To do this, I have developed relationships with fishermen firsthand.

Having worked with some of these same suppliers for thirty or forty years, I've been able to deliver the best seafood possible because as I said, it's about trusting your source, which comes with time and consistency. These guys care—and so do I. They take pride in their work. We are loyal to each other and there's a real integrity factor. These are people my wife and I have gotten to know over the years—we visit them, we share meals with them, and we've even vacationed with some of them. I know their families too, because many of these are family-run businesses.

Throughout the book, I've highlighted some of these fishermen with photos taken during my visits. I want you to see that these are REAL people following best practices. These people are not just my seafood suppliers. During certain seasons, I speak to these guys daily. I've developed long-distance relationships with them, and over time, they've become my friends.

Opposite page, clockwise from upper-left: Jerry Gault with Joe; Nireus Fish Farm; Lee Fish; Joe with the Nolan Family in Montauk; Sarah and Steve Malinowski; Kissy Bridges with Joe; Joe with Willy Phillips; Joe and Magnus Skretting in Norway; Howard Pickerell and Joe inspecting oysters

GRILL

YELLOWFIN TUNA

"JOE SAYS

I'm going to start you off grilling with the easy fish first. Tuna and swordfish are the two best starter grilling fish because their textures are not delicate but dense and meaty, similar to a piece of beef. These fish grow big, up to hundreds of pounds, so it makes it possible to cut nice thick steaks. And everyone knows how to cook a steak, right? Well, at least most people do. And guess what? Cooking tuna and swordfish steaks is similar to cooking beef steaks, except it takes less time. (Hello, they're called STEAKS aren't they?!)

RECIPES

—

SEARED
TUNA STEAKS

SERVES 4

¼ cup **extra-virgin olive oil**, plus more for brushing the grates

4 (6- to 8-ounce) **skinless tuna steaks**, cut 1 inch thick

Sea salt and **freshly ground pepper** to taste

Suggested Side:
Sautéed Broccoli Rabe
(page 217)

GUIDE TO
TUNA COOKING TIME

RARE
1 to 1½ minutes per side
(red in the middle)

MEDIUM-RARE
3 minutes per side
(pink in the middle)

WELL-DONE
4½ minutes per side
(gray in the middle)

Tuna is one of the best fish for grilling. Sear it over a nice hot fire and you'll get caramelized grill marks that create somewhat of a crust with raw, juicy meat inside. Cooking tuna is like cooking beef: Rare is red in the middle, medium-rare is pink in the middle, and well-done is gray in the middle. I definitely suggest rare. (If you're squeamish about eating rare or raw fish, turn to The Myth of "Sushi Grade" on page 190.)

Preheat your stovetop grill pan or outdoor grill over the highest heat. Brush or spray the grates with oil.

Rinse the fish and pat it dry with paper towel. Put the tuna steaks in a large bowl and drizzle with the olive oil (I always do this!). Using your hands, gently rub the oil over the steaks until they're fully coated. Season with salt and pepper.

Place the fish on the preheated grill and cook to your desired doneness using the times in the chart to the left, flipping the fish only once. Resist the temptation to flip sooner than the time given, or it will stick. Remove the fish from the grill and serve.

GRILLED SWORDFISH STEAKS

The best part of grilling your own fish is that YOU ARE IN CONTROL! I find that many people overcook swordfish, and it gets dry. But when you grill a large swordfish steak rare for just a few minutes per side, you get a juicy, flavorful, meaty result that even non-fish lovers can appreciate. Swordfish is available year-round because it's caught in all parts of the world, including South Africa and Australia. In the summer months, mainly August and September, we get it locally here in Atlantic waters.

Preheat your stovetop grill pan or outdoor grill over the highest heat. Brush or spray the grates with oil.

Rinse the fish and pat it dry with paper towel. Put the steaks in a large bowl and drizzle with the olive oil. Using your hands, gently rub the oil over the steaks until fully coated. Season with salt and pepper.

Place the fish on the preheated grill and cook to the desired doneness, 2½ to 3 minutes per side for rare (4 minutes per side for medium-rare and 5 minutes per side for well-done). Be patient and resist the temptation to flip sooner, or it will stick. Remove the fish from the grill and serve.

SERVES 4

¼ cup **extra-virgin olive oil**, plus more for brushing the grates

4 (8-ounce) **swordfish steaks**, cut 1 inch thick

Sea salt and **freshly ground pepper** to taste

Suggested Sides: Grilled Zucchini (page 237) and Crispy Stovetop New Potatoes (page 231)

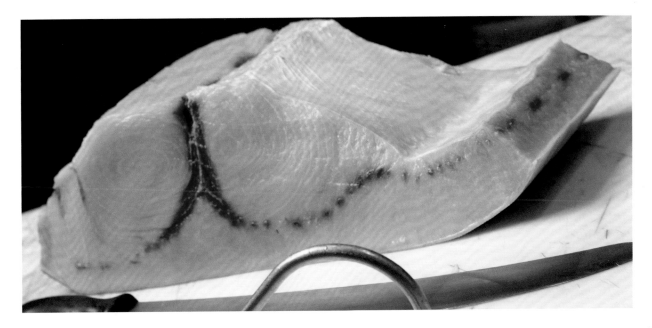

FLAME-COOKED NORWEGIAN
SALMON STEAKS

SERVES 4

¼ cup **extra-virgin olive oil**, plus more for brushing the grates

4 (6- to 8-ounce) **skin-on Norwegian salmon steaks** with the center bone

Sea salt and **freshly ground pepper** to taste

The sole difference between a salmon steak and a fillet is the cut. Because salmon are big fish, they can be cut perpendicular to the spine, which is how you get a steak. It's like a cross section of the fish with a bone in it. Fillets, on the other hand, are cut parallel to the spine and are boneless. I included the steak because it's an old tradition, an aesthetic thing. I'm going to guess you'll never hear of a salmon steak twenty years from now. But I do know for certain that if you can cook a burger, you can cook a salmon steak.

Preheat your stovetop grill pan or outdoor grill over the highest heat. Brush or spray the grates with oil.

Rinse the fish and pat it dry with paper towel. Put the salmon steaks in a large bowl and drizzle with the olive oil. Using your hands, gently rub the oil over the steaks until fully coated. Season with salt and pepper.

Place the salmon on the preheated grill. Cook for 2 minutes per side for rare (3 minutes per side for medium-rare and 4 minutes per side for well-done). Be patient and resist the temptation to flip sooner, or it will stick. Remove the fish from the grill and serve.

FIRE UP YOUR GRILL GAME

Gas or charcoal? They both have their place, but I prefer charcoal because it gets hotter than a gas flame. Hot grates are ideal for searing fish. I also like the flavor food gets from an open fire.

But if you don't have an outdoor grill, you can still get the delicious flavors that result from browning food by grilling inside. I use a cast-iron French grill (see Sources, page 249).

And either way, indoor or out, greasing your grates is a must! If you don't do it, your fish will stick. Always oil your grill before fish touches it. To do this, use a folded paper towel dipped in a food-grade oil and, holding it with tongs, liberally rub the grates. You can use a spray oil, but if there's a flame, be careful because it may flare up.

GRILLED ORGANIC
SALMON FILLETS

Fish are not manufactured like boxes of candy. Whether salmon are wild or farmed, they are from nature so their taste and texture can differ (see Wild Versus Farmed Fish, page 117). The question as to which is better is complex, and I'm not here to resolve it. I can tell you that both are an excellent source of omega-3 fatty acids—and both are delicious. You can use either wild or farmed for grilling, but it will depend on the time of year. The season for wild salmon runs March through September.

Preheat your stovetop grill pan or outdoor grill over the highest heat. Brush or spray the grates with oil.

Rinse the fish and pat it dry with paper towel. Put the fillets in a large bowl and drizzle them with the olive oil. Using your hands, rub the oil evenly all over both sides of the fish. Season with salt and pepper.

Place the salmon on the preheated grill flesh-side down first to prevent sticking. Cook for 2 minutes per side for rare (3 minutes per side for medium-rare and 4 minutes per side for well-done). Be patient and resist the temptation to flip sooner or it will stick. Remove the fish from the grill and serve.

SERVES 4

2 tablespoons **extra-virgin olive oil**, plus more for brushing the grates

4 (6- to 8-ounce) **skin-on organic salmon fillets**

Sea salt and **freshly ground pepper** to taste

Suggested Side: Corn & Edamame Salad (page 225)

"
JOE
SAYS
___

Organic salmon is always farm-raised. Wild salmon cannot be organic certified because their feed is not controlled.

LOCAL BLUEFISH ON THE GRILL

2 teaspoons **extra-virgin olive oil**, plus more for brushing the grates

4 (6- to 8-ounce) **skin-on bluefish fillets**

Sea salt to taste

Suggested Side: Sautéed Broccoli Rabe (page 217)

Beware: if your palate is new to fish, bluefish is not the smooth merlot of seafood. Bluefish is more akin to a big, bold cabernet. It has a reputation of being oily and pungent, which is not completely unwarranted. Its flavors *are* strong, but not as intense as say, a northern mackerel. Trust me on this: bluefish is one of the most flavorful fish you'll ever taste. As its name infers, it's a beautiful blue color when raw that turns opaque white when cooked. Look for bluefish when they're in season, which is the summer months for those of us on the East Coast. Another bonus, it's relatively inexpensive!

Preheat your stovetop grill pan or outdoor grill over the highest heat. Brush or spray the grates with oil.

Rinse the fish and pat it dry with paper towel. Put the fillets in a large bowl and drizzle them with the olive oil. Using your hands, rub the oil evenly all over both sides of the fish. Season with salt.

Place the fish flesh-side down on the preheated grill and cook for 2 to 3 minutes per side, or just until the meat turns opaque white. Resist any temptation to flip sooner, or the skin will stick. Serve immediately.

YES, YOU CAN EAT FISH SKIN

If you're scared of fish skin, don't be. Think of it like chicken skin. Would you eat the skin off a poached chicken? No way. However, the golden skin of a roast bird is irresistible, like that of a roast fish. One of my favorite fish skins is that from a seared salmon, which happens to be rich in omega-3 fatty acids, making it good for your heart.

If you're going to eat the skin, make sure your fishmonger scales the fish, which they will most likely do if you ask them to clean the fish.

You can eat almost all types of fish skin, but do note there are a few that are inedible, including tuna, swordfish, and skate skin. And make sure those you do eat are nice and crispy—because that's when they taste best!

CRISPY WHOLE
MEDITERRANEAN
BRANZINO,
recipe page 42

CRISPY WHOLE
MEDITERRANEAN BRANZINO

SERVES 2

2 tablespoons **extra-virgin olive oil**, plus more for brushing the grates and for serving

2 (1-pound) **whole branzini,** cleaned

Sea salt to taste

2 to 4 sprigs fresh **rosemary**

Thirty years ago you found this wild Mediterranean fish only in southern European countries. In Italy it's called *branzino*, in France it's known as *loup de mer*, in Greece *lavraki*, and in Portugal *robalo*. Today it's probably the second most popular upscale farmed fish in the world, after salmon. While it still swims wild, the farmed variety is delicious too. Neither bland like tilapia nor strong like bluefish, the flavor is acceptable to the majority of palates.

Preheat your stovetop grill pan or outdoor grill over the highest heat. Brush or spray the grates with oil.

Rinse the fish and pat them dry with paper towel, both inside and out. Put them in a large bowl and drizzle with the olive oil. Using your hands, rub the oil evenly all over both sides of the fish and inside the bellies. Season with salt and place the rosemary inside the bellies.

Place the fish on the preheated grill and cook for 5 minutes. Then, using tongs, carefully pick the fish up by the head, flip it over, and grill for another 5 minutes. Whatever you do, don't move it. Don't touch it. Just wait the entire 5 minutes, then drizzle with olive oil to finish and serve immediately.

WHOLE-FISH PHOBIA

When I've served whole fish to guests, I've been asked more than once if I can debone it for them. What don't they understand? It's a whole fish. WHOLE! I just put a whole fish on everyone's plate and let them eat it how they want. I encourage you to do the same. Believe me, people get over their whole-fish phobia fast and learn to navigate around bones when they're hungry. I may sound tough, but I know they can do it, and of course I'm always there to help. Again, the goal is for everyone to feel comfortable with fish. If you want to do the work for your guests, see How to Fillet a Whole Grilled Fish on page 245 or go to citarella.com, and I'll show you how to fillet a fish after you've cooked it.

When I order a *whole* fish in a restaurant and it comes boned, to me, that's not whole! Hello? Many restaurants here in America cater to the percentage of the population who don't like bones—or heads or tails for that matter— which is a shame, because those parts have purpose. During cooking, the bones help protect the flesh, keeping it moist and juicy, which is true with most any meat.

JOE SAYS

Fresh fish should be vibrant and firm. The belly sticks out of an old fish, just like the belly of an old man, which is a sign not to buy it.

GRILLED WHOLE PORGY

SERVES 2

2 tablespoons **extra-virgin olive oil**, plus more for brushing the grates

2 (1-pound) **whole porgies**, cleaned

Sea salt and **freshly ground pepper** to taste

Suggested Sides: Roasted Cauliflower (page 224) and Sautéed Green Beans (page 235)

In my opinion, porgies are one of the best-tasting fish in the ocean. The delicate, white-fleshed meat is almost sweet, like the ever-popular red snapper. I believe it would be as well-known as snapper if it didn't have so many bones, which is why porgies are almost always sold whole. It's really time-consuming to remove all the bones from the fillet—it's like plucking a chicken! Don't let a few bones get in the way of trying this tasty catch though. I say, go whole or go home!

Preheat your stovetop grill pan or outdoor grill over the highest heat. Brush or spray the grates with oil.

Rinse the fish and pat them dry with paper towel, both inside and out. Put them in a large bowl and drizzle with the olive oil. Using your hands, rub the oil evenly all over both sides of the fish and gently inside the bellies. Season with salt and pepper.

Place the fish on the preheated grill and cook for 5 minutes. Then, using tongs, carefully pick the fish up by the head, flip it over, and grill for another 5 minutes. Whatever you do, don't move it. Don't touch it. Just wait the entire 5 minutes, then serve immediately.

HOT-OFF-THE-GRILL
PORTUGUESE SARDINES

SERVES 4 AS AN
APPETIZER

Unlike branzino or porgy, sardines are not for rookies. Their flavor is intense. But if you like a rich fish taste, it's worth seeking out fresh, plump sardines from Portugal, which are the best in my opinion. If you're thinking of canned sardines right now, don't. You'll recognize Portuguese sardines by their size: they're bigger than the tinned variety—and so much better tasting. A light coating of Wondra flour helps crisp up the silvery skin and seal in the flavorful juices. Each fish becomes so succulent, you'll want to eat 'em hot off the grill. The meat just falls off the tiny bones in tender flakes.

Canola, grapeseed, or other high-heat cooking oil, for brushing the grates

8 **whole sardines** (about 1½ pounds), cleaned with heads left on

Sea salt to taste

¼ cup **Wondra flour** or **all-purpose flour**

Pink Hawaiian sea salt for garnish (optional)

Preheat your stovetop grill pan or outdoor grill over the highest heat. Brush or spray the grates with oil. Line a rimmed baking sheet with paper towels.

Rinse the fish and pat them dry with paper towel. Lay the fish on the prepared baking sheet and lightly sprinkle both sides of the fish with salt, then dust with the flour to coat. Turn the fish over and coat the other side with flour, shaking off any excess.

Place the fish on the preheated grill and cook for 2 minutes per side, or until slightly charred and browned, resisting any temptation to flip sooner or the skin will stick. Sprinkle with pink salt if desired for garnish. Serve immediately.

TENDER
EAST COAST CALAMARI

SERVES 4

3 tablespoons
**extra-virgin olive
oil**, plus more for
brushing the grates

12 (4- to 6-inch)
whole calamari
(bodies and
tentacles), cleaned

Sea salt and
**freshly ground
pepper** to taste

Microgreens,
for garnish

ASK YOUR
FISHMONGER

*for whole cleaned
calamari bodies and
whole tentacles.*

Just like I tell you not to overcook fish, the same is true for all types of seafood. Don't get distracted—not even for a minute—or your meal may be ruined. Calamari needs to be grilled quickly or it'll get chewy, like a tire. Rubbing both the tentacles and the bodies with olive oil is key. It'll help keep the moisture in, again preventing unwanted chewiness. Get the timing right and you'll bring out a naturally sweet and mild ocean flavor.

Preheat your stovetop grill pan or outdoor grill over the highest heat. Brush or spray the grates with oil.

Rinse the calamari and pat them dry with paper towel. Put the calamari bodies and tentacles in a large bowl and drizzle with the olive oil. Using your hands, gently rub the oil over the bodies and tentacles until fully coated. Season with salt and pepper.

Place the lightly oiled calamari bodies and tentacles on the preheated grill. After 2 minutes, flip the tentacles, and after 3 minutes, flip the bodies. Be PATIENT and resist the temptation to flip sooner. Cook for another 2 and 3 minutes, respectively. Remove from the grill, garnish with microgreens, and serve immediately.

JOE SAYS

"I use the words *squid* and *calamari* interchangeably, but in my opinion *calamari* sounds sexier.

GRILLED SPANISH
BABY OCTOPUS

If you've never seen a baby octopus before, their leggy bodies and purple color are quite impressive. I've had people tell me octopus meat is tough. I briefly cook the octopus in boiling water before searing it on the grill, so it becomes tender and you're not chewing for days. They have a sweet taste and still have a slightly chewy but not rubbery texture. They're not always readily available at fish markets though. Look for them in specialty fish stores or in Spanish or Italian markets. I serve these as an appetizer, but they're also delicious thrown over a bed of greens for a light lunch, in which case this recipe will serve two.

Bring a pot of water to a boil over high heat. Place the octopi in the boiling water and cook for 5 minutes. Drain and let cool.

Preheat your stovetop grill pan or outdoor grill over the highest heat. Brush or spray the grates with oil.

Place the octopi in a large bowl and drizzle with the olive oil. Using your hands, gently rub the oil over the bodies and tentacles until fully coated.

Place the whole octopi on the preheated grill. Cook for 3 minutes. Be patient and resist the temptation to flip before the 3 minutes is up. Then, using a spatula or tongs, flip each octopus and cook for another 3 minutes. (If your octopi are closer to 16 ounces each, cook them for 5 minutes per side.) Cut the octopi into bite-size pieces and season with salt to taste. Serve immediately.

SERVES 4 AS AN APPETIZER

2 (8- to 16-ounce) **whole baby octopi**, cleaned

2 tablespoons **extra-virgin olive oil**, plus more for brushing the grates

Sea salt to taste

NORTH ATLANTIC
WATERS
& Beyond

Being from New York, *I am very lucky to have many species of seafood at my fingertips, including Atlantic cod, whiting, porgy, striped bass, fluke, calamari, bluefish, clams, scallops, and my favorite, shad. My proximity is one reason I've had so much experience with these fish and speak about them confidently. If I were from Florida or California, I wouldn't have the access to or availability of all of these species locally.*

Because of developments in transportation and packaging, many of these fish are now widely available in other parts of the US as well. Fish farming has also contributed to the variety of fish available year-round. Advancements in the seafood industry have made it possible for you and me to enjoy fresh fish from all over the country and the world.

Take the salmon industry, for example, which has changed significantly from when I started in the business. Fresh salmon was only available seasonally, March through September. Come October, the only choice was frozen, and you'd have to wait until the following spring for fresh salmon again.

The Food Revolution (see page 18), which started in the '70s, was the beginning of farmed salmon. Suddenly, fresh salmon was available twelve months a year.

To give a more mainstream example, there was actually a time when we couldn't get berries year-round. I know it seems hard to imagine for those of you who are under forty because we can now access most anything we want when we want it, but it's true. Seems like the dark ages—I call it the pre-radicchio era—when iceberg and romaine dominated the produce sections, not the wide variety of lettuces we have available today.

Because of these developments in food growing, handling, packaging, and transportation, we can now enjoy grouper from Florida, sardines from Portugal, and branzino from Greece to name a few. Throughout the book, I refer to over 35 different species of fish. I encourage you to be flexible with your choices. If you go to the market with the goal of buying porgy, but the fishmonger tells you branzino is the best that day, follow his or her lead. The fishmonger knows which fish came into the store when. I like to think of it like shopping at the farmer's market. See what the farmer brings in, *then* make your decision. Do the same with your fishmonger.

A MALE CRAB
is identified by its long, pointy apron shape

A FEMALE CRAB
is identified by its round apron shape

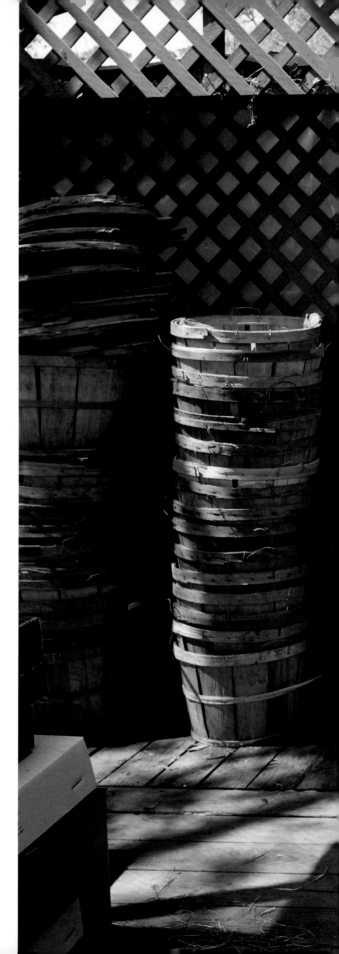

GAULT SEAFOOD

Beaufort, South Carolina

JERRY GAULT, a waterman whose family has been in the business for generations, is a commercial crabber in South Carolina I've worked with for over thirty years. Before Jerry, getting live soft-shell crabs from the South to New York was tough. The attention he takes with the care of crabs ensures we get truly "soft" shells. He puts a lot of effort into the process. At his facility, starting in March, depending on water temperature, his team of "shedders" works around the clock to pull crabs from the tanks while they molt (see page 97 to read more about soft-shell crabs).

BAKE
&
ROAST

FLUKE

RECIPES

—

OVEN-ROASTED
LITTLENECK CLAMS

**SERVES 4 AS AN
APPETIZER**

2 dozen **raw
littleneck clams**,
cleaned, shucked,
shells reserved (see
How to Shuck Clams,
page 245)

¼ cup **seasoned
breadcrumbs**

2 tablespoons **extra-
virgin olive oil**

**ASK YOUR
FISHMONGER**

*to shuck the clams,
place them in a container
with the juice, and
save the shells for you.
Refrigerate until use
(see Joe Says, page 121).*

You know those stuffed clams served in restaurants with 42 pounds of stuffing on them? These are NOT those. I want you to taste the sweet, tender clam, not the stuffing. Otherwise it's a waste. I sprinkle breadcrumbs on shucked clams and there you have it, a delicious appetizer—and you don't have to send a search party out for the clam!

Preheat the oven to 375°F.

Line a rimmed baking sheet with parchment paper and arrange the clam shells, open-side up, on the baking sheet. Place one clam in each shell. Set aside.

In a small bowl, combine the breadcrumbs with the olive oil and toss until they are thoroughly moistened. Top each clam with a small mound of the breadcrumb mixture. It is important that you can still see the clam (remember, you want to taste the clam, not mask the flavor).

Bake the clams in the preheated oven for 8 to 10 minutes, until the breadcrumbs are golden brown. Serve immediately.

PARMIGIANO-DUSTED BAKED OYSTERS

Sprinkle fresh oysters with finely grated Parmesan cheese, put them in the oven, and you've got one delicious indulgence. The cheese creates a lightly browned crust that prevents the briny liquor from evaporating, keeping the oyster smooth and silky. Remember, you never want to mask the flavor of seafood, only enhance it. You can use any type of oyster for this recipe. A trayful of these makes a great appetizer for a crowd.

Preheat the oven to 375°F. Line a rimmed baking sheet with parchment paper and arrange the oyster shells, open-side up, on the baking sheet. Place one oyster in each shell. Lightly sprinkle the cheese over each oyster.

Bake the oysters in the preheated oven for 9 minutes. Serve immediately.

" JOE SAYS

Oysters come from all over the world. There are hundreds of varieties. I've eaten them from the Indian Ocean, the Mediterranean, the Atlantic, and the Pacific. They vary some in taste, salinity, and texture—one not being better than the other. It's all personal preference. If you want to compare them, you need to do it side by side. If you taste one this week, and another next week, you're never going to know the difference. And to enjoy an oyster, chew it, don't rush through it.

SERVES 2 AS AN APPETIZER

1 dozen **raw oysters**, cleaned, shucked, shells reserved (see How to Shuck Oysters, page 244)

½ cup finely grated **Parmesan cheese**

ASK YOUR FISHMONGER

to shuck the oysters, place them in a container with the juice, and save the shells for you. Refrigerate until use.

OVEN-ROASTED
MONTAUK TILEFISH

SERVES 2

2 (6- to 8-ounce) **skin-on Montauk tilefish fillets**

2 tablespoons **extra-virgin olive oil**

Sea salt and **freshly ground pepper** to taste

Suggested Side: Sautéed Green Beans (page 235)

We get tilefish locally here in New York off the coast of Montauk, of which a good portion is caught year-round. These beauties, with their distinctive golden spots, are as delicious as they are gorgeous. The fish bakes up nicely with a thin layer of oil, which helps the pearly white lean meat with a nice flake stay moist. You rarely see it on menus though because it's just not as well-known as other big game fish. If you spot it at your fish market, grab it!

Preheat the oven to 375°F. Line a rimmed baking sheet with parchment paper and set aside.

Rinse the fish and pat it dry with paper towel. Put the tilefish in a large bowl and drizzle with the olive oil. Using your hands, gently rub the oil over the fillets until fully coated. Season with salt and pepper.

Place the tilefish skin-side up on the prepared baking sheet. Bake for 8 to 10 minutes, or until just cooked through. Serve immediately.

BAKED COD

Historically, cod has been a mainstay in Atlantic waters and a part of European diets for hundreds of years. The fish also played a big part in North American history. Today, cod is still popular, and the flaky, firm meat is sweet and mild enough to convert even the most skeptical non-fish eaters.

Preheat the oven to 375°F. Line a rimmed baking sheet with parchment paper and set aside.

Rinse the fish and pat it dry with paper towel. Put the fillets in a large bowl and drizzle with the olive oil. Using your hands, gently rub the oil over the fish until fully coated. Season with salt and pepper and sprinkle with the herbes de Provence.

Place the cod on the prepared baking sheet. Bake for 8 to 10 minutes, or until just cooked through. Serve immediately.

SERVES 2

2 (6- to 8-ounce) **skinless cod fillets**

2 tablespoons **extra-virgin olive oil**

Sea salt and **freshly ground pepper** to taste

2 teaspoons **herbes de Provence**

Suggested Side: Sautéed Spinach (page 236)

" JOE SAYS

For easy cleanup after baking fish, do yourself a favor and always line your baking sheet with parchment paper.

ROASTED FLUKE

SERVES 2

2 (8-ounce) **skinless fluke fillets**

2 tablespoons **extra-virgin olive oil**

Sea salt and **freshly ground pepper** to taste

Suggested Side: Crispy Stovetop New Potatoes (page 231)

You can cook just about any mild, white-flesh fish using this technique. It's great for beginners. Rub with a little olive oil and seasoning, put it in the oven for a few, and you've got a healthy, delicious protein in minutes. Pair it with a side or two like Crispy Stovetop New Potatoes (page 231) or Sautéed Green Beans (page 235), and you've got a healthy, wholesome dinner on the table in just under an hour (skip the potatoes and it'll only take 15 minutes). Now that's fast! Cooking fish is really NOT intimidating, but actually very simple.

Preheat the oven to 375°F. Line a rimmed baking sheet with parchment paper and set aside.

Rinse the fish and pat it dry with paper towel. Place the fluke fillets in a large bowl and drizzle with the olive oil. Using your hands, gently rub the oil over the fish until fully coated. Season with salt and pepper.

Place the fluke onto the prepared baking sheet and bake for 8 minutes, or until just cooked through. Serve immediately.

STUFFED CALAMARI

It's become tradition that I cook the Feast of Seven Fish for friends on Christmas Eve. But if you know me, I don't stop at seven. No way. I cook something more like ten or eleven dishes, and this stuffed calamari is always one of them. Turn to page 74 to read more about the other dishes I serve on this special night.

Preheat the oven to 375°F. Heat 1 teaspoon of the oil in a medium sauté pan over medium-high heat. Add the mushrooms and cook for about 3 minutes, or until slightly tender. Set aside in a medium bowl.

Heat another teaspoon of the oil in the pan and sauté the calamari tentacles for 3 minutes. Let the tentacles cool and chop them into ½-inch pieces.

Add the tentacles to the bowl with the sautéed mushrooms, the breadcrumbs, the remaining ¼ cup oil, and salt and pepper to taste. Stir to combine. The stuffing mixture should be moist.

Using your fingers, stuff the body of each calamari with the mushroom mixture, being careful not to pack it too tightly. Thread a toothpick through the open end of each calamari to keep it closed.

Cover the bottom of an 8- by 10-inch baking dish with 1 cup of the marinara sauce and place the calamari snugly in the dish. Top with the remaining marinara sauce and bake in the preheated oven for 40 minutes. Remove the toothpicks before serving. Sprinkle with chopped chives for garnish if desired.

This dish reheats well the next day: cover the baking dish with foil and heat the calamari in a 350°F preheated oven for 15 minutes.

SERVES 4

2 teaspoons plus ¼ cup **extra-virgin olive oil**, divided

8 small **white mushrooms**, trimmed, cut into ¼-inch pieces

8 (4- to 6-inch) **whole calamari** (bodies and tentacles), cleaned

½ cup **seasoned breadcrumbs**

Sea salt and **freshly ground pepper** to taste

1½ cups **marinara sauce**, store-bought or homemade (page 241), divided

Chopped **chives**, for garnish

ASK YOUR
FISHMONGER

for whole cleaned calamari bodies and whole tentacles.

WHOLE CLEANED
CALAMARI

STUFFED
CALAMARI.

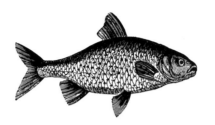

JOE'S

FEAST

of SEVEN

FISH

There don't seem to be any hard and fast rules about this Italian Christmas Eve tradition, which is celebrated in many ways. This is a good thing, because as I've said before, I'm not big on rules. When I hear "seven fish," I don't want to be limited. I go big—I always go for more. Part of it is that I love to feed people. It makes me happy to see a big smile after someone eats a scallop for the first time. Or to see someone reluctant to try a grilled sardine or an oyster shooter shake her head in disbelief at how tasty it is—and see her reach for another. Maybe it's the Italian in me, but maybe it's also the fact that I know seafood can have a broader appeal than it gets credit for.

I cook a version of this dinner every Christmas Eve, rotating between different pasta dishes year to year. I always include a few fried seafood items and a few baked ones, and never is there a year without my signature stuffed calamari. You certainly don't need to be Italian, or even celebrate Christmas, to cook up this feast—you just need to love fish, and lots of it, which hopefully you do by now!

My menu traditionally includes any combination of the following:

Oyster Shooters (page 182)

Sautéed Nantucket Bay Scallops (page 101)

Crispy Calamari (page 146)

Fried Shrimp (page 149)

Merluzzo Fritti (page 150)

Sautéed Skate (page 107)

Grilled Smelts

Hot-off-the-Grill Portuguese Sardines (page 47)

Oven-Roasted Littleneck Clams (page 60)

Parmigiano-Dusted Baked Oysters (page 63)

Stuffed Calamari (page 71)

Insalata di Mare (page 134)

Baccala

Shrimp Scampi

Plus any one of these:

Spaghetti with Crab Sauce

Fettuccine with Lobster Sauce

Pasta with White Sauce Using Scrod and Lobster Stock

Spaghetti Vongole (page 164)

Linguine Bottarga (page 167)

BROIL

SNAPPER

RECIPES

—

BROILED
FLORIDA RED SNAPPER

SERVES 4

¼ cup **extra-virgin olive oil**, plus more for greasing the pan

4 (6- to 8-ounce) skin-on Florida **red snapper fillets**

2 teaspoons **smoked paprika**

Sea salt and **freshly ground pepper** to taste

Suggested Sides: Sautéed Broccoli Rabe (page 217) and Crispy Stovetop New Potatoes (page 231)

" JOE SAYS

If you put your fish in a large bowl while you oil it, you're more likely to coat all of the fish and have less chance of it sticking. This is a good time to season your fish also.

With its trademark crimson-colored skin, wild-caught American red snapper has a mildly sweet but distinctive flavor. Its semi-firm meat is lean and moist. Here, the meat gets a little color from the paprika and a slight char from the broiler.

Preheat the broiler on high and place a rack 5 to 6 inches from the flame. Lightly coat a rimmed baking sheet with olive oil.

Rinse the fish and pat it dry with paper towel. Put the fillets in a large bowl and drizzle with the olive oil. Using your hands, gently rub the oil over the fillets until fully coated. Sprinkle with the paprika and season with salt and pepper.

Place the snapper skin-side up on the prepared baking sheet and broil for 6 minutes without flipping. Transfer the fish to warm plates and serve.

BLACKENED
SWORDFISH STEAKS

While grilling is probably one of the most popular methods for cooking swordfish, broiling also does this meaty, satisfying fish justice—especially in the winter, when you don't want to go outside to light the grill. Cook this steak rare and you may find yourself comparing it to the meatiness of a beef strip steak. It's just as juicy as beef when cooked medium-rare (still pink on the inside). And not to keep repeating myself, but there's no fear in eating rare fish as long as it's extremely fresh. To spice things up a bit, I rub smoked paprika or a Cajun spice blend (where paprika is the main ingredient) on the fish to add another dimension.

Preheat the broiler on high and place a rack 5 to 6 inches from the flame. Lightly coat a rimmed baking sheet with olive oil.

Rinse the fish and pat it dry with paper towel. Season the steaks with salt and pepper, then rub them all over with the paprika.

Place the swordfish on the prepared baking sheet and broil without flipping for 6 minutes for rare (7 minutes for medium-rare and 8 minutes for well-done). Serve immediately.

SERVES 4

Olive oil, for greasing the pan

4 (8-ounce) **skinless swordfish steaks**, cut 1 inch thick

Sea salt and **freshly ground pepper** to taste

2 teaspoons **smoked paprika** or **Cajun spice blend**

Suggested Sides: Chunky Mashed Potatoes (page 230) and Tomato & Red Onion Salad (page 234)

" JOE SAYS

This recipe uses a dry rub so don't oil the fish.

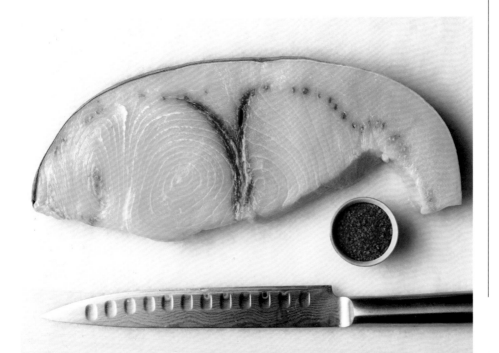

THE
NOLAN
FAMILY

Montauk, New York

THE SAME WAY I've developed relationships with crabbers, I depend on the fish guys at Lockwood & Winant, our wholesale division, to create relationships in their own areas. One of those connections I appreciate most was created by salesperson Anthony Bencivenga with the Nolan family, who we've been working with for almost thirty years. Owners John and Laurie have been building their family business for decades. They both come from fishing backgrounds and have continued the tradition of catching tilefish off the coast of Montauk for generations. This family is close-knit, and their son, Young John, captains their 82-foot boat, Sea Capture. Standing on the dock in Montauk, watching them unload their golden-spotted catch, is an impressive sight.

BROILED FLUKE
WITH HERBES DE PROVENCE

SERVES 2

2 tablespoons **extra-virgin olive oil**, plus more for greasing the pan

2 (6- to 8-ounce) **skinless fluke fillets**

Sea salt to taste

2 teaspoons **herbes de Provence**

Suggested Side: Grilled Asparagus (page 216)

" JOE SAYS

Cooking a fish fillet is probably one of the quickest, easiest—and most delicious—dinners you can make. That is, if you pay attention to timing. Overcook a fillet by as little as 30 seconds, and you may ruin it. (Remember, DON'T YOU DARE PICK UP YOUR PHONE!)

There are dozens of species of flatfish, among them plaice, grey sole, flounder, and fluke. The differences in the lean meat are subtle, and in most cases the fish are interchangeable for cooking purposes. Adding herbes de Provence—a classic herb mix made up of any number of herbs including basil, fennel, marjoram, tarragon, rosemary, thyme, and lavender—complements the mild flavor of the fish. Most grocery stores carry herbes de Provence already blended, but you can always use a few pinches of each herb to make your own combination.

Preheat the broiler on high and place a rack 5 to 6 inches from the flame. Lightly coat a rimmed baking sheet with olive oil.

Rinse the fish and pat it dry with paper towel. Place the fluke fillets on the prepared baking sheet and drizzle with the olive oil. Season with salt and rub the herbes de Provence evenly over both sides of the fillets.

Broil for 5 minutes without flipping, or until just cooked through. Serve immediately.

SEASONAL
BONED SHAD

Shad is a big deal in upstate New York. Well-known for its roe, which is considered a delicacy, it was once one of the most important fish commercially caught in the Hudson. One of the last true seasonal seafood items, shad can be found from Florida to upstate New York, swimming up freshwater rivers and streams to spawn in the spring. With one of the highest fat contents of all fish, shad has a rich, distinctive flavor, a tender, almost creamy texture, and also a good dose of omega-3s. Because the meat has such a high fat content, there's no need to oil the fish as I usually instruct. And note, the length of the ingredient list is NOT a typo. This fish is so full of flavor, it needs nothing else.

Preheat the broiler on high and place a rack 5 to 6 inches from the flame. Lightly coat a rimmed baking sheet with oil.

Rinse the fish and pat it dry with paper towel.

Place the shad skin-side down on the prepared baking sheet. Be sure to leave the fish fillet "closed." (When the fillets are boned, there are two "flaps" that fold closed. Leave them closed to prevent overcooking.) Broil the fillets for 5 minutes without flipping. Taste and season with salt accordingly; you may not need any. Serve immediately.

SERVES 4

Extra-virgin olive oil or **grapeseed oil**, for greasing the pan

4 (6- to 8-ounce) boneless, **skin-on shad fillets**

Sea salt to taste (optional)

Suggested Side: Sautéed Brussels Sprouts & Mushrooms (page 221)

" JOE SAYS

Shad is one of the boniest fish in the sea, so be sure to ask for it boned. The very specific way of removing the bones is a dying art—very few fishmongers know how to do it, but we do. Let's hope yours does too. If not, call me!

BROILED
NOVA SCOTIA LOBSTER

SERVES 2

2 (1¼-pound) **whole live Nova Scotia lobsters**

2 tablespoons **extra-virgin olive oil**, divided

"
JOE
SAYS
—

Make sure your lobsters are moving when you buy them. When you get the live lobsters home, do not put them in water. Just keep them in the refrigerator covered with a damp newspaper or paper towel.

Fast and healthy, broiling is one of the best ways to cook seafood. Here the direct heat of the flame sears the lobster meat, keeping it juicy while giving it a little bit of color. Unless you've got a commercial oven, you can probably only broil one, maybe two lobsters at a time, so don't take on broiling for a party or gathering—try grilling instead. A few boiled corn cobs add some color to the platter as well.

Preheat the broiler on high and place a rack 5 to 6 inches from the flame. Line a rimmed baking sheet with foil.

First, pith (or kill) the live lobster. Place the lobster on its back on a cutting board and insert the tip of a sharp chef's knife into the center of its body, and with one swift motion, slice lengthwise, upward toward the eyes, cutting straight through the head and between the eyes. Rotate the lobster, and again insert the knife into the center; repeat the same motion, splitting the lobster toward the tail end. The lobster will continue to move slightly, but this is just a nerve response. Once it's split, crack the lobster apart like you're breaking the spine of a book so it lays open flat. Repeat with the second lobster.

Remove any rubber bands or binders from the claws. Lay one lobster flesh-side up on the prepared baking sheet. Brush the visible meat of the lobster with 1 tablespoon of the olive oil.

Broil the lobster for 8 minutes, or just until the meat is no longer translucent. (It's actually okay to eat it when it's translucent—better than overcooking it!) Remove from the oven and repeat the oiling and broiling with the second lobster and the remaining olive oil. See page 246 for how to remove cooked lobster meat from the shell.

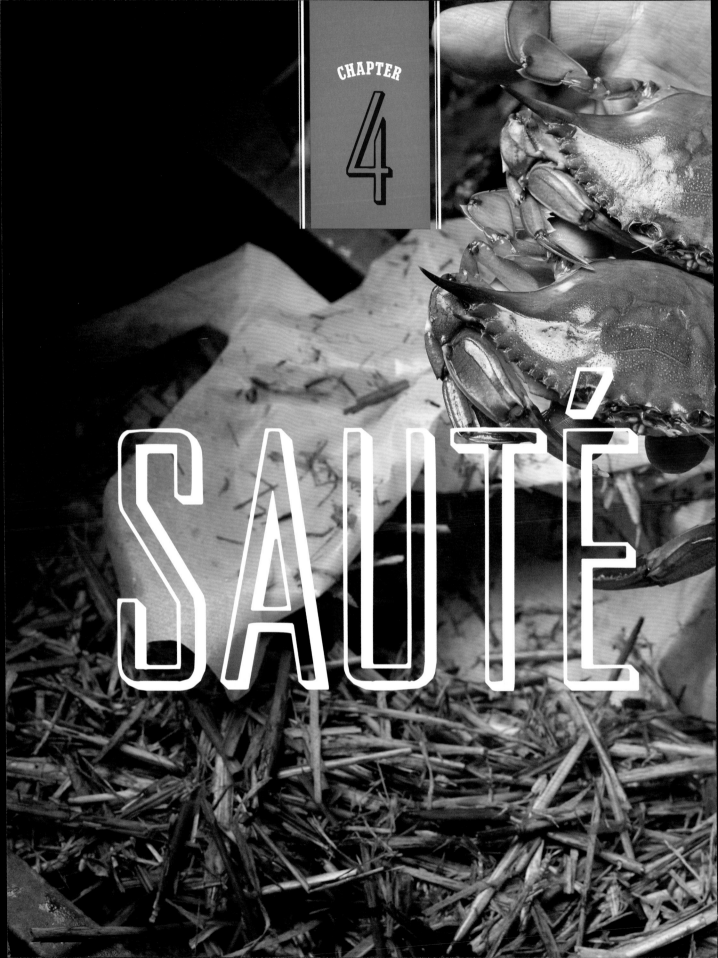

SAUTÉ

SOFT-SHELL CRABS

RECIPES

—

HELLO!?

Yes, you eat the whole crab. If you've never had a soft-shell crab, you have to get it past your brain that you really can eat the claws and all.

SAUTÉED
SOFT-SHELL CRABS

SERVES 2

4 **whole live soft-shell crabs**, cleaned

½ cup **Wondra flour** or **all-purpose flour**

About ½ cup **extra-virgin olive oil**

Sea salt and **freshly ground pepper** to taste

Ask me what seafood I like best and I'll tell you I love it all. Press me for an answer and I'll admit that one of my favorites is soft-shell crabs. On the East Coast, soft-shell crabs are available early March through September. Crabs are caught in a pot, then put into open saltwater tanks, where they can be observed as they shed their shells. This is a time-sensitive process. They have people watching 'round the clock because the crabs shed at all times and have to be pulled from the water shortly thereafter—if not they become a hard-shell crab. These crustaceans can molt up to an impressive twenty-three times in eighteen to twenty-four months. Lightly sautéed, they turn golden and sweet, and the briny meat stays juicy. What could be better? The key...don't overcook the crab. The goal is to get the soft-shell exterior nice and crispy while keeping the meat plump and tender. And yes, you eat the WHOLE thing!

ASK YOUR
FISHMONGER

for whole, live, cleaned soft-shell crabs, which should be cooked within 24 to 48 hours—and ideally sooner.

Rinse the crabs with cold water and pat them dry with paper towel.

Dust the crabs with flour by sprinkling a light layer onto each side and shaking off any excess.

Pour a very thin layer of olive oil into a large shallow skillet and heat over medium heat until it starts to shimmer. Sauté the crabs for 1½ to 2 minutes per side. Sprinkle with salt and pepper to taste. Serve immediately.

SEARED SEA SCALLOPS

SERVES 4

12 (1- to 1½-inch-wide) **raw sea scallops**

2 tablespoons **extra-virgin olive oil**

Sea salt to taste

Microgreens, for garnish

"

JOE
SAYS
—

Don't buy scallops stored in a milky white fluid. It's either a chemical preservative (the term is "wet scallops"), or it means the scallops are old—milky liquid is the first sign to STAY AWAY! Look for a fishmonger who sells "dry scallops."

Delicate and creamy with a sweet caramelized crust, seared sea scallops are one of the best things you can eat. The trick to achieving the perfect sear is twofold: be sure to pat the scallops dry before cooking, and don't be afraid to get the pan nice and hot. Scallops are plump and tender when cooked correctly. Remember, a HOT, HOT pan is the secret.

Pat the scallops dry with paper towel, then put them in a large bowl and drizzle with the olive oil. Using your hands, gently toss with the oil until fully coated.

Preheat a large sauté pan over HIGH HEAT. Once it's hot, sear the scallops until golden, 1 to 1½ minutes per side. Season to taste with salt and garnish with microgreens. Serve immediately.

SAUTÉED NANTUCKET
BAY SCALLOPS

Nantucket bay scallops, the most coveted of all the Atlantic scallops, are smaller (they're about the size of a thimble) and more tender than sea scallops. These little delicacies are so sweet, I eat them raw like candy. That's not for everyone though, so try a quick sear, which brings out the smooth, buttery flavor. Their season here in the Northeast is short—November through March—so be sure to look out for them during that time. You can substitute Peconic bay scallops here too.

Pat the scallops dry with paper towel and season them with salt.

In a medium sauté pan over high heat, warm the olive oil until it starts to shimmer. Briefly shake the pan as you add the scallops. The friction from the scallops moving in the pan will prevent them from sticking. At this point, don't touch them; let them sear and caramelize to golden brown, about 2 minutes total. Serve immediately.

SERVES 4

2 pounds **raw Nantucket bay scallops**

Sea salt to taste

1½ tablespoons **extra-virgin olive oil**

<blockquote>
" JOE SAYS
—

You know that old saying about guests? That, like fish, they begin to smell after three days? That's fresh fish. The bones, shells, and waste—they don't go quite so long. So take any seafood waste out of the house right after cooking, or it will start to smell.
</blockquote>

PAN-COOKED
RAZOR CLAMS

SERVES 2

1 pound raw **razor clams**

2 tablespoons **panko** (Japanese breadcrumbs)

Sea salt and **freshly ground pepper** to taste

1 tablespoon **extra-virgin olive oil**

4 **garlic cloves**, finely chopped

The shape, texture, and taste of these is not your typical rounded clam. I can't tell you why the shell resembles a straight-edge razor. If you need to know, call 1-800-GOD for the answer. I will tell you, though, razor clams are tender with an almost al dente texture. I find these clams sweeter than other kinds. When buying them, look for clams that are nearly, but not entirely, closed. There should be a small gap in the shell opening, and most of the meat should be inside the shell. If you see that the shell is wide open and the whole clam is hanging out, don't buy them!

Put the clams in a colander or directly in the sink and rinse them thoroughly (use a sink sprayer if you have one). Set aside. Heat a large sauté pan over medium heat. Add the panko, season with salt and pepper to taste, and cook, stirring often, until lightly toasted, about 1 minute. Remove the breadcrumbs from the pan and set aside.

In the same pan, heat the oil and garlic over medium heat until the garlic starts to turn golden, about 2 to 3 minutes. Add the clams. Cover and cook for 2 to 3 minutes, or until the clam shells open.

Transfer the clams to individual serving plates, removing the top shell. Sprinkle each clam with the toasted panko and serve immediately.

ENDURANCE SEAFOOD

Nags Head, North Carolina

ANOTHER GUY I've been working with for decades is Murray Bridges, owner of Endurance Seafood in Nags Head, North Carolina. Once a backyard business, his company is now the largest crab dealer in the Outer Banks. Murray's family has worked for generations in the crab industry, and he now works side by side with his daughter Kissy, who continues to run the operation. After many years in the business, Murray still goes out on his boat every day. He gave his business the right name, because after 70 years he's still supplying crabs up the East Coast—he certainly has endured.

ASK YOUR
FISHMONGER

*to fillet the skate by
removing the cartilage.*

SAUTÉED SKATE

You'll most likely never see a whole skate at a fish counter. It looks like a stingray, but you only eat the meat from the wings. The mild, nutty flesh has a ribbed texture that I personally love. It's local and plentiful to us here in the Northeast, so it's reasonably priced. You'll find it worldwide though, including in the Mediterranean Sea and even the Arctic Ocean.

Rinse the skate and pat it dry with paper towel. Dust the fillets on both sides with flour to coat. Shake off any excess.

Pour 2 tablespoons of the oil into a large, heavy sauté pan, adding more if needed to coat the bottom of the pan. Place over medium-high heat and, when the oil starts to shimmer, put two fillets in the pan. Do not overcrowd the pan. Sear the skate until it is golden brown and caramelized, about 3 minutes per side.

Sprinkle liberally with salt. Repeat the cooking process with the remaining oil and fillets. Serve hot.

SERVES 4

4 (6- to 8-ounce)
boneless, skinless skate fillets

½ cup **Wondra flour**
or **all-purpose flour**

About 4 tablespoons
extra-virgin olive oil, divided

Sea salt to taste

ASK YOUR
FISHMONGER

*for whole cleaned
calamari bodies and
whole tentacles.*

JOE'S
ITALIAN SURF & TURF

SERVES 4

3 to 4 tablespoons
extra-virgin olive oil

3 pounds ripe
heirloom **tomatoes**,
cut into eighths

Sea salt and
**freshly ground
pepper** to taste

½ pound **sweet
Italian sausage,**
removed from casings

½ pound **spicy
Italian sausage,**
removed from casings

1 pound cleaned
calamari, bodies cut
into ½-inch rings and
tentacles cut in half

A few years ago, my wife and I were staying with friends in Florida, and they were craving a good, hearty Italian supper. I wanted to make them one of my signature dishes, but I couldn't find the ingredients so I called Citarella to have the sausage and calamari overnighted (you can do this too . . . it isn't just my luxury!). So even though we had to wait a day for the ingredients, we didn't have to wait much longer to eat because this comforting combination comes together in about 30 minutes, though it tastes like it's been simmering all day. I like to eat it as is, but for an even more satisfying meal, serve it over pasta.

Heat the oil in a large sauté pan over medium-low heat. Add the tomatoes, cover, and cook, stirring occasionally, until the tomatoes soften, about 10 to 15 minutes. Season with salt and pepper to taste.

Using your hands, crumble the sausage meat into the pan with the tomatoes and stir to combine. Break apart any larger pieces of meat with a wooden spoon. Next add the calamari and stir to combine.

Cover the pan and cook for 7 to 9 minutes, stirring occasionally, until the sausage is cooked through and the calamari starts to shrink (surprisingly, the calamari doesn't get overcooked). Then remove the lid and let the liquid reduce until the sauce thickens slightly, about another 2 to 3 minutes. Taste the sauce and adjust the seasoning, if necessary. Serve as is, or spoon it over cooked rice or pasta.

SAUTÉED
WILD STRIPED BASS FILLETS

Striped bass is popular for its robust flavor and large, flaky texture. The fillets are nice and thick because the wild striped bass sold in New York are regulated and need to be between 28 and 38 inches in length, which means the fish are a good size. Conservation works.

Rinse the fillets and pat them dry with paper towels. Dust the fish on both sides with flour to coat. Shake off any excess, then season with salt and pepper.

Pour the oil into a large, heavy sauté pan, adding more if needed to coat the bottom of the pan. Heat over medium heat and, when the oil starts to shimmer, put the fillets flesh-side down in the pan and cook for about 3 to 4 minutes per side for a 1-inch-thick fillet (a 2-inch-thick fillet will need 5 to 6 minutes per side). Be patient and resist the temptation to flip sooner, and only flip once. Serve immediately.

SERVES 4

4 (8-ounce) **skin-on wild striped bass fillets**, cut about 1 inch thick

½ cup **Wondra flour** or **all-purpose flour**

Sea salt and **freshly ground pepper** to taste

2 tablespoons **extra-virgin olive oil**

Suggested Sides: Sautéed Corn & Tomato Salad (page 226) and Roasted Fennel (page 227)

POACH

&

STEAM

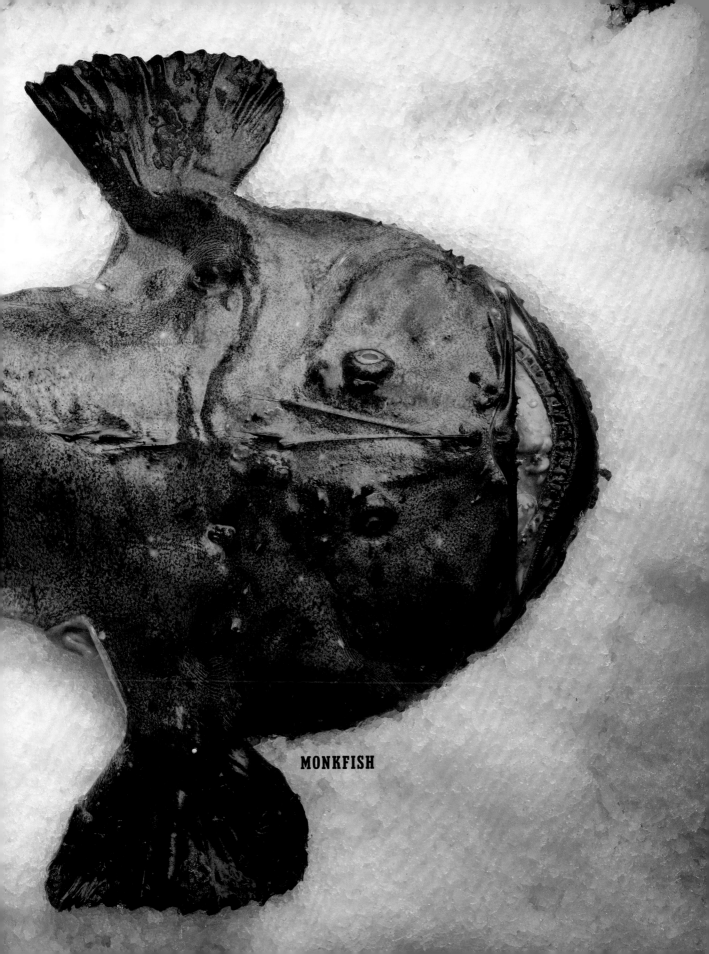

MONKFISH

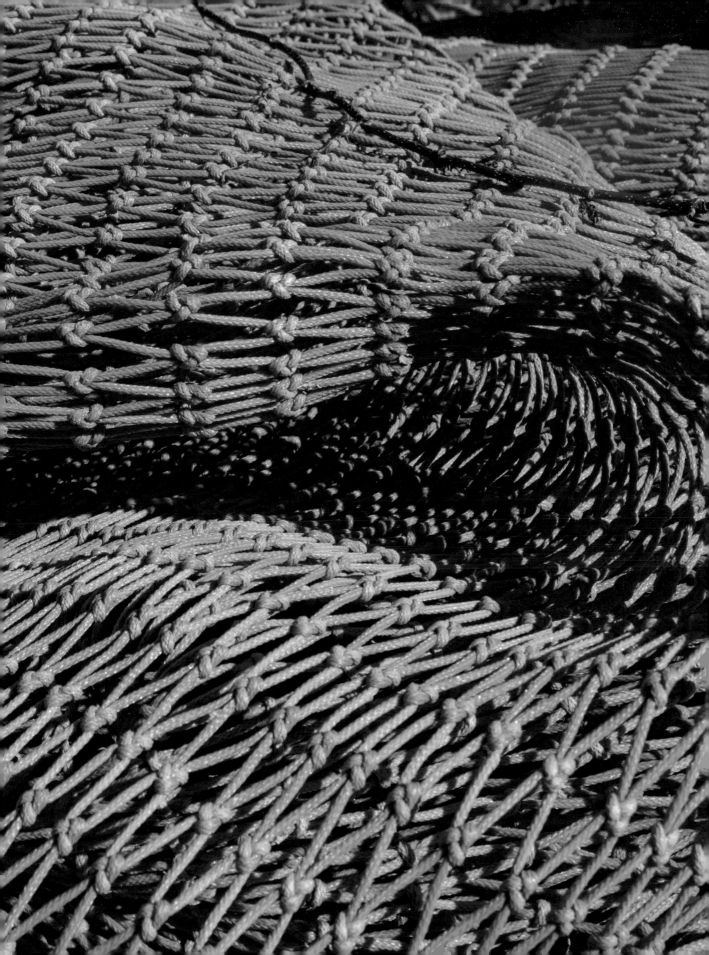

RECIPES

—

POACHED SALMON

2 (6- to 8-ounce) **skin-on salmon fillets**

Sea salt and **freshly ground pepper** to taste

1 teaspoon **extra-virgin olive oil**

Creamy Dill Sauce (page 240), for serving (optional)

Suggested Side: Sautéed Spinach (page 236)

If there's a particular preparation for salmon that's versatile, it's poaching. You can serve poached salmon many ways—for brunch alongside eggs, during summer in a salad, or in winter paired with Sautéed Spinach (page 236) and Potato Purée (page 233). You can also serve it chilled, at room temp, or even warm, which is when it's especially rich and buttery-tasting. The outcome is almost always elegant but requires little effort, and the cleanup is just as easy.

Rinse the fish and pat it dry with paper towel. Season the fillets with salt and pepper.

Lightly coat the bottom of a large sauté pan with the oil to prevent sticking. Add ¼ inch of water to the pan and bring the water to a simmer over medium-high heat. Gently slide the fillets skin-side down into the pan.

Cover the pan and cook for 3 to 5 minutes, depending on the thickness of the fillets and the desired doneness (3 to 4 minutes if you prefer a rare fillet and 4 to 5 minutes if you like it more cooked). Serve at desired temperature with dill sauce if you'd like.

WILD VERSUS FARMED FISH

I'm constantly being asked which is better, wild or farmed fish. My answer: they both can be excellent. Notice that I said "can." Just like there are responsible chicken farmers who uphold the highest animal-welfare standards, there are fish farmers who follow sustainable and responsible practices. Know your source. Do some research. Check out NOAA's fishwatch.gov. Ask your fishmonger where they get their fish and how it's being treated. You can know what farmed fish are being fed, but do you know what wild fish are eating? My point: there's no hard and fast answer. Ecosystems change, farming practices change. Do a side-by-side comparison for taste to see which you prefer.

STEAMED FLOUNDER
WITH ITALIAN SEASONING

Now, you may think all Italian mothers can cook. My mother was great at many things, but not in the kitchen. I do have fond memories of her making this flounder though—and it was her favorite—which makes it dear to me. The difference between her flounder and mine: mine starts out as a 6-ounce fillet and goes to a 5-ounce fillet. Her flounder would start at 6 ounces but end up as 2 ounces because she'd steam it too long. THAT'S WHY I TELL YOU TO TIME YOUR FISH. Follow my timing, and you'll end up with wonderfully moist meat.

Rinse the flounder and pat it dry with paper towel. Season the fillets with the Italian seasoning and salt and pepper.

Coat the bottom of a large sauté pan with the olive oil. Add ¼ inch of water to the pan and bring to a simmer over medium-high heat. Gently slide the flounder into the pan, keeping some space between the two fillets. Cover the pan and lower the heat so the water continues to simmer. Cook the fillets for 3 minutes. Using a fish spatula, remove the fillets from the pan and serve immediately.

SERVES 2

2 (6- to 8-ounce) **skinless flounder fillets**

1 teaspoon **Italian seasoning**

Sea salt and **freshly ground pepper** to taste

1 teaspoon **extra-virgin olive oil**

Suggested Sides: Sautéed Spinach (page 236) and Tomato & Basil Bruschetta topping (page 218)

CLAMS & MONKFISH
BRODETTO

SERVES 4

4 dozen **raw littleneck clams** (see Joe Says, page 133)

2 tablespoons **extra-virgin olive oil**

16 **garlic cloves**, finely minced

½ cup **dry white wine**

1½ pounds **skinless monkfish fillet**, cut into 1-inch pieces

One Sunday I was home alone watching a game. Most guys order wings or cook up nachos when they watch football. Not me. Instead, my mind went straight to *vongole*, or clams. Come on, where else would you expect a fish guy's thoughts to go? But instead of tossing the wine-steamed clams with pasta, I paired them with monkfish—the flesh is so sweet and dense that many compare it to lobster. A light, delicious *brodetto* (Italian for "broth") develops from the fish and seafood juices. Genius if I do say so myself. It's certainly special enough to serve at a dinner party.

Put the clams in a colander or directly in the sink and rinse them thoroughly (use a sink sprayer if you have one). Set aside.

Heat the olive oil in a large, heavy saucepan over low heat and add the garlic. Sauté for 2 to 3 minutes, or until the garlic turns light golden brown.

Add the clams and wine and cover the pan. Increase the heat to medium-high and steam the clams until they open, about 8 minutes. Using tongs, remove the open clams, still in their shells, from the pot and set aside. There may be some clams that take longer to open than others, so continue cooking those for a few more minutes. After that, discard any clams that do not open.

Increase the heat if needed to bring the clam broth back to a gentle simmer, add the monkfish to the pan, and cover. Allow the fish to cook in the broth for 5 minutes. Transfer the fish, clams, and broth to a large serving bowl or four individual bowls. Serve hot.

JOE SAYS Never store raw clams in a sealed plastic bag or container because they will suffocate (a good fishmonger will pierce the plastic bag if the clams are sold to you in one). Instead, keep raw clams in a bowl in the refrigerator for up to 48 hours.

When steaming or poaching fish, never flip it. And always be sure to place it in the pan skin-side down.

STEAMED
FLORIDA GROUPER

A mild, dense fish, grouper comes from the South Atlantic, so you'll often see it on menus in Florida and as a mainstay throughout the Caribbean. It was once available only in those areas, but with developments in packaging and shipping, it's now distributed worldwide. A simple steam ensures this fish stays moist while bringing out the pure, natural flavors of the creamy-tasting meat.

Rinse the fish and pat it dry with paper towel. Season the fillets with salt and pepper.

Coat the bottom of a large sauté pan with the olive oil. Add ¼ inch of water to the pan and bring to a gentle boil over medium-high heat. Once boiling, gently slide the fillets skin-side down into the pan in a single layer.

Cover the pan and cook the fillets for 6 minutes, or until just cooked through. Using a fish spatula, remove the fillets from the pan and serve immediately. Drizzle with olive oil and sprinkle with parsley for garnish if desired.

SERVES 2

2 (8- to 10-ounce) **skin-on Florida grouper fillets**, cut ½ inch thick

Sea salt and **freshly ground pepper** to taste

1 tablespoon **extra-virgin olive oil**, plus more for serving

Chopped **parsley**, for garnish (optional)

Suggested Side: Lentil Salad (page 228)

POACHED WILD STRIPED BASS

WITH TOMATO & GARLIC

SERVES 2

2 (8-ounce) **skin-on wild striped bass fillets**, cut 1 inch thick

Sea salt to taste

1 tablespoon **extra-virgin olive oil**, plus more for serving

1 cup **Tomato & Basil Bruschetta topping** (page 218)

Striped bass is a chef's favorite because it's a hearty fish that cooks up silky and sweet. I love it because it's rich, and even though the meaty flakes hold up well with many preparations, poaching makes them even more moist and consistent. Topping the fish with bright red tomatoes and fragrant garlic gives the poached fillets some contrasting color and flavor. It also quickly turns this simply prepared fish into a meal.

Rinse the fillets and pat them dry with paper towel. Season the fish with salt.

Coat the bottom of a large sauté pan with the olive oil. Add ¼ inch of water to the pan and heat over medium-high heat. When the water comes to a gentle boil, gently slide the fillets skin-side down into the pan in a single layer.

Cover the pan and lower the heat to a simmer. Cook the fillets for 5 to 6 minutes, or until just cooked through. Using a fish spatula, remove the fillets from the pan and transfer to serving plates. Spoon ½ cup bruschetta topping over each fillet and drizzle with olive oil. Serve immediately.

WHOLE STEAMED LOBSTER

I once went to a steakhouse where they tried to sell me a whole 6-pound lobster. It sounds decadent, but I would never buy it. In fact, I would never buy one bigger than 2½ pounds. You know why? Because there's no way you can cook a large lobster like that evenly. Some parts will cook faster than others. Stick with smaller lobsters to keep the cooking even and easy.

Fill a wok-style pan with 1 inch of water and set over high heat. Once the water starts to simmer, pick one lobster up by the middle, remove any binding on the claws, and put it in the pan, tucking the tail under if needed to make it fit. Cover the pan and cook for 8 minutes. (For a larger, 2¼-pound lobster, cook for 12 minutes.) Using tongs, remove the lobster from the pan and rinse under cold water. Repeat the process with the second lobster.

When the lobsters have cooled to the touch, put one on a cutting board, insert a knife into the middle of the back, and pull the knife toward the tail. Turn the lobster around and insert the knife back into the middle and cut toward the head. Pull the lobster apart, take the sac out, and discard. Then remove the meat from the claws and the tail (see page 246). Eat immediately or refrigerate until ready to serve.

SERVES 2

2 (1¼-pound)
live lobsters
(see Joe Says,
page 90)

" JOE SAYS

The colder the water, the better the fish or seafood. The fat content is higher and you get more meat percentage-wise from cold-water fish—in this case lobster.

WHAT'S THAT GREEN STUFF?

Have you noticed that green paste in a lobster (see page 246)? It's called tomalley and it's a substance that acts as the liver and pancreas. Some people are turned off by the green stuff, but I never pass up the chance to eat this rich, creamy delicacy with its intense lobster taste. Don't hesitate to suck the small side claws or other parts of the shells either. You won't regret it.

WHOLE STEAMED
LOBSTER,
recipe page 127

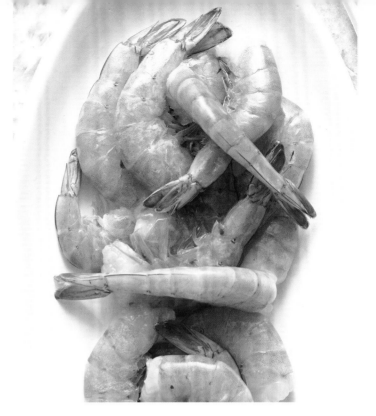

" JOE SAYS

Have you ever noticed the black, string-like vein that runs along the back of a shrimp? It's actually not a vein but the shrimp's digestive tract. Sometimes they're big, other times you may hardly notice them. It won't hurt you to eat one, they just look unappetizing (see page 246 for How to Devein Shrimp).

CLASSIC SHRIMP COCKTAIL

This is seafood cooking 101. Nail this recipe and you're well on your way to understanding how seafood should really be cooked. People usually cook shrimp for ten minutes or more. No way, don't do it. I'm asking for your full concentration here. Ready? When you cook large shrimp, you add it to boiling water, look at the clock, and time it for two minutes. No reboil. That's it. You're done. There's nothing like perfectly tender, sweet shrimp with a subtle briny flavor. That wasn't hard, was it? Remember, your fishmonger can peel and devein the shrimp if you ask, but see page 246 if you want to learn how to devein them yourself.

Fill a medium pot with 1 inch of water and bring it to a boil over high heat. Meanwhile, fill a large bowl halfway with cool water and set aside.

Once the water boils, add the shrimp. Cover and cook for 2 minutes. Immediately drain the shrimp and transfer them to the bowl of cool water to stop the cooking process. Season the shrimp by salting the cool water and stirring the water slightly. When the shrimp are cool, drain them and serve with cocktail sauce (or if you're like me, don't).

SERVES 4

24 **raw large shrimp** (about 16 to 20 per pound), peeled and deveined (see page 246)

Sea salt to taste

Cocktail sauce, store-bought or homemade (page 240), for serving (optional)

SICILIAN-STYLE
CLAMS

SERVES 4

2 dozen **raw littleneck clams** (see Joe Says, page 121)

6 tablespoons **extra-virgin olive oil**, divided

12 **green beans**, trimmed, cut into 1-inch pieces

Sea salt and **freshly ground pepper** to taste

6 **garlic cloves**, finely chopped

½ cup **dry white wine**

1 recipe **Chunky Mashed Potatoes** (page 230), hot

1 tablespoon drained **capers**

2 tablespoons freshly squeezed **lemon juice** (from about 1 small lemon)

One of the best parts of traveling is discovering new foods. Clams over mashed potatoes was one such find when my wife and I stumbled upon a nice little restaurant in Palermo. This recipe is a nod to that unexpected pairing we ate—and to my Sicilian roots. The lemon and capers mixed into the potatoes is especially fresh, and when combined with my memories of a vacation by the sea, this recipe is a definite keeper. Note, if you make the potatoes first, they will stay warm when left covered in a pan on the stovetop, as the rest of the dish comes together quite quickly.

Put the clams in a colander or directly in the sink and rinse them thoroughly (use a sink sprayer if you have one). Set aside.

Heat 2 tablespoons of the olive oil in a medium sauté pan over medium. Add the green beans and season with salt and pepper to taste. Sauté the beans for 1 to 2 minutes, or until they're soft with a slight crunch. Remove the beans from the pan and set aside.

Heat the remaining olive oil in a large, heavy saucepan over low heat and add the garlic. Sauté for 2 to 3 minutes, or until the garlic turns light golden brown.

Add the clams and the wine and cover the pan with a lid. Increase the heat to medium-high and steam the clams until they open, about 8 minutes. Using tongs, remove the open clams, still in their shells, from the pot. Set aside. There may be some clams that take longer to open than others, so continue cooking those for a few more minutes. After that, discard any clams that do not open.

Put the mashed potatoes in a bowl and stir in the capers and lemon juice. Spoon the mashed potatoes onto a serving platter. Place the steamed clams in their shells on the potatoes and scatter the sautéed green beans over the clams and potatoes. Spoon some of the clam cooking broth over the top to finish. Serve immediately.

INSALATA DI MARE (SEAFOOD SALAD)

SERVES 4

3 teaspoons **sea salt**, divided

¾ pound **raw large shrimp** (16 to 20 per pound), peeled and deveined

1 **whole baby octopus** (about ¾ pound), cleaned

¾ pound **calamari**, cleaned, bodies cut into ¾-inch rings and tentacles left whole

¾ pound **conch** meat, precooked

¼ cup **extra-virgin olive oil**

4 to 5 teaspoons freshly squeezed **lemon juice** (from about ½ large lemon)

3 to 4 **garlic cloves**, crushed

1 tablespoon chopped **flat-leaf parsley**

Freshly ground pepper and/or **red pepper flakes** to taste

This traditional Italian dish is all about the variety of textures you get from the combination of several types of seafood, which are marinated with olive oil and a few cloves of garlic for a light finish. While most seafood is best prepared à la minute, this dish holds up nicely in the refrigerator when made in advance.

Cook the shrimp: Fill a large sauté pan half full with water, add 1 teaspoon salt, and bring to a boil over medium-high heat. Lower the heat, then add the shrimp and simmer for 2 minutes. Remove immediately from the heat, drain, and run under cold water to stop the cooking. Roughly chop the shrimp into bite-size pieces, discarding the tails. Set aside.

Next, cook the octopus: Fill the sauté pan again half full with water, add 1 teaspoon salt, and bring to a boil over medium-high heat. Lower the heat, then add the octopus and simmer for 8 to 10 minutes. Remove from the heat, drain, and run the octopus under cold water to stop the cooking process. Slice the body into quarters and then chop it into bite-size pieces. Set aside.

Lastly, cook the calamari: Fill the sauté pan half full with water, add 1 teaspoon salt, and bring to a boil over medium-high heat. Lower the heat, then add the calamari and cook both the rings and tentacles for 3 to 5 minutes. Remove from the heat, drain, and run the calamari under cold water to stop the cooking process.

Slice the precooked conch meat into ¾-inch-thick pieces. Set aside.

In a large bowl, whisk together the olive oil and lemon juice until it emulsifies, then stir in the garlic and parsley. Season with salt and pepper (and pepper flakes, if desired) to taste. Add the cooked seafood and toss to combine. This can be served right away, at room temperature, and it is also good the next day out of the refrigerator.

" JOE

SAYS

You know those big shells you put up to your ear? That's conch (pronounced konk), also called scungilli in Italian. In order to get the meat out, the whole shell needs to be boiled. So know that any conch you buy out of the shell is already cooked, and there's no need to cook it again. Confirm with your fishmonger though to be sure.

ASK YOUR

FISHMONGER

for whole cleaned calamari bodies and whole tentacles, cooked conch meat, cleaned octopus, and peeled and deveined shrimp.

INSALATA
DI MARE,
recipe page 134

JOE SAYS

When you buy mussels, they are alive. Make sure the shells are closed tightly, which is a sign of freshness, before you cook them. If any are partially open, tap them, wait a few seconds, and they should close. Never store raw mussels in a sealed plastic bag or container because they will suffocate (a good fishmonger will pierce the plastic bag if the mussels are sold to you in one). Instead, keep raw mussels in a bowl in the refrigerator for up to 48 hours.

WHITE WINE–STEAMED MUSSELS

This is our go-to dinner after a long day at the beach because it only takes minutes to prepare. Sharing a big pot of plump mussels with friends—plus some crusty Italian bread to soak up the garlicky broth and a bottle (or two) of rosé—is exactly how I like to spend warm summer nights.

Rinse the mussels thoroughly, remove any beards (the black bristly strands sticking out of the shell), and make sure that no sand remains. Set aside.

Coat the bottom of a stockpot or Dutch oven with the olive oil and heat over low. When the oil is warm, add the garlic and sauté until it just starts to turn golden, about 2 minutes.

Add the mussels and the wine to the pot, increasing the heat slightly so the wine just starts to simmer, cover, and steam until the mussels open, about 5 to 8 minutes. If you overcook the mussels they can shrivel to a quarter of their size. You want to stop cooking them once they open, so don't hesitate to remove the open ones from the pot with tongs while the others continue to cook. There can be a few that take longer than others, but discard any mussels that do not open. Divide the mussels between four serving bowls and ladle warm broth over them. Serve with crusty bread on the side.

SERVES 4

4 pounds **Prince Edward Island mussels**

2 tablespoons **extra-virgin olive oil**

16 **garlic cloves**, finely minced

½ cup **dry white wine**

Crusty Italian bread, for serving

FRY

MERLUZZO
(WHITING)

RECIPES

—

WHY
FRY?

———

BECAUSE ANYTHING FRIED TASTES GOOD—well, most anything, and certainly seafood!

I find that people shy away from fried foods for two reasons: 1) cooking with oil scares them and 2) health reasons. My answers: 1) If you can boil water, you can boil oil and 2) if the temperature is hot enough, it seals the seafood and not much oil is actually absorbed.

When frying, always use an oil with a high smoking point, like grapeseed or canola, which are also low in saturated fats. If you have a candy thermometer, use it. The ideal temperature is 375°F—watch it like a hawk. If the oil isn't hot enough, your seafood will end up tasting greasy. When you cook your seafood in batches, be sure to let the oil come back to temperature before doing the next round.

Because I fry a lot, I invested in a home deep fryer. I use a Waring Pro model, but there are many on the market. I like deep-frying better than stovetop frying because it's cleaner—the mess is more contained—and you don't need a thermometer. I also like using the baskets—they're easier and feel more like a professional kitchen! Plus, the fryer holds a good amount of oil.

My frying recipes call for 2 quarts of oil, which should create a depth of about 2 inches of oil in an 8-inch pot. If your pot is bigger, use more oil (or conversely, if your pot is smaller, you can get away with 1 quart of oil). Some people prefer frying in oil deeper than 2 inches, so please feel free to use more. This is the minimum amount of oil that I feel achieves my desired result. The key is never to overcrowd the pot. Always fry in small batches—there should be some space between items for them to move around.

And one little tip: dredge seafood in flour right before you're about to fry it. If you do it hours in advance, the flour will become soggy and won't crisp up.

CRISPY CALAMARI

2 quarts **canola**, **grapeseed**, or other **high-heat cooking oil**, for frying

½ cup **Wondra flour** or **all-purpose flour**

2 pounds **calamari**, cleaned, bodies sliced into ½-inch rings and tentacles left whole

Sea salt to taste

Microgreens, for garnish

Marinara sauce, store-bought or homemade (page 241), for serving (optional)

ASK YOUR FISHMONGER

for whole cleaned calamari bodies and whole tentacles.

In order to get the crispiest golden-brown coating on calamari, I always recommend frying in small batches. If you overcrowd the pan, the temperature of the oil can drop and the calamari can get soggy. When the oil is good and hot, the calamari fries up quickly and soaks up very little, if any, oil.

Pour the oil into a large pot, Dutch oven, or fryer. It should be at least 2 inches deep. Heat the oil to 375°F. If you don't own a candy or oil thermometer, simply sprinkle a pinch of flour into the oil. If it sizzles, it's ready.

Meanwhile, put the flour in a shallow dish. Pat the calamari dry with paper towel and dredge it in the flour, shaking off any excess.

When the oil is hot, using a slotted spoon or spider, fry one test piece of calamari to ensure your oil is at the correct temperature. If your test is successful and the calamari is pale golden and crispy, lower a small batch of calamari into the oil and fry for 2 minutes, then transfer to a plate or baking sheet lined with paper towels to drain. Sprinkle liberally with salt. Repeat the process with the remaining calamari, continuing to fry in small batches, and letting the oil return to temperature before frying the next batch. Serve hot, garnished with microgreens, and with a small side of marinara for dipping, if desired.

ONE SHRIMP, TWO SHRIMP, **HOW MANY SHRIMP IN A POUND?**

Good question, because there's no hard and fast rule. What one store sells as jumbo, another may sell as large. "Shrimp count" determines the size of the shrimp. The fewer shrimp in a pound, the larger the size of the shrimp.

Here's a point of reference: At Citarella we sell large shell-on shrimp, 16 to 20 in a pound; medium shell-on shrimp, 31 to 35 in a pound; and jumbo shell-on shrimp, 10 or less per pound.

If you're looking for a certain number of shrimp, it's better to order how many you need versus a pound amount.

FRIED SHRIMP

I like to keep things casual when my wife and I are entertaining. Even though we have a dining room, everyone always ends up hanging out in the kitchen. Especially when I'm frying. Guests stand around the counter waiting to get the golden, crispy shrimp straight from the fryer. Can you blame them? They are best when they're hot.

Pour the oil into a large pot, Dutch oven, or fryer. It should be at least 2 inches deep. Heat the oil to 375°F. If you don't own a candy or oil thermometer, simply sprinkle a pinch of flour into the oil. If it sizzles, it's ready.

Meanwhile, put the flour in a shallow dish. Rinse the shrimp and pat them dry with paper towel. Dredge the shrimp in the flour, shaking off any excess.

When the oil is hot, using a slotted spoon or spider, lower a small batch of shrimp into the oil and fry for 2 minutes, then transfer to a plate or baking sheet lined with paper towels to drain. Sprinkle liberally with salt. Repeat the process with the remaining shrimp, continuing to fry in small batches, and letting the oil return to temperature before frying the next batch. Serve hot.

SERVES 4

2 quarts **canola, grapeseed,** or other **high-heat cooking oil**, for frying

½ cup **Wondra flour** or **all-purpose flour**

2 pounds **raw large shrimp** (about 16 to 20 per pound), peeled and deveined (see page 246)

Sea salt to taste

MERLUZZO FRITTI
(FRIED WHITING)

SERVES 4

2 quarts **canola**, **grapeseed**, or other **high-heat cooking oil**, for frying

1 cup **Wondra flour** or **all-purpose flour**

2 pounds whole **merluzzo (whiting)**, filleted and cut into 1½-inch chunks

Sea salt to taste

"

JOE
SAYS
___

Serve deep-fried seafood right away. The longer you wait to eat it, the more it loses its intensity and crunch.

We always serve this traditional Italian dish as part of our Feast of Seven Fish, which, true to its name, is always a feast (see page 75 for my official menu offerings). This flaky, light fish cooks up perfectly crisp on the outside and moist on the inside when it's deep-fried. Cut it into small pieces before frying and serve it on a platter with cocktail forks.

Pour the oil into a large pot, Dutch oven, or fryer. It should be at least 2 inches deep. Heat the oil to 375°F. If you don't own a candy or oil thermometer, simply sprinkle a pinch of flour into the oil. If it sizzles, it's ready.

Meanwhile, put the flour in a shallow dish. Rinse the merluzzo and pat it dry with paper towel. Dredge the pieces of fish in the flour, shaking off any excess.

When the oil is hot, using a slotted spoon or spider, lower a small batch of the fish into the oil and fry for 3 minutes, then transfer to a plate or baking sheet lined with paper towels to drain. Sprinkle liberally with salt. Repeat the process with the remaining fish, continuing to fry in small batches, and letting the oil return to temperature before frying the next batch. Serve hot.

FRIED OYSTERS & LITTLENECK CLAMS

For some reason, when I fry, I like to cook up a bunch of things. It becomes "Fry Night." Once you've got the oil hot, it's kind of like, why not? It's so easy and fast, and it gives a little variety. Two of my favorites are oysters and clams. But don't fry them together. The oysters take 15 seconds more, and I mean it, 15 seconds is it! DON'T WALK AWAY or even think about cracking open a beer. Wait until after you take them out of the oil, *then* enjoy them together.

Pour the oil into a large pot, Dutch oven, or fryer. It should be at least 2 inches deep. Heat the oil to 375°F. If you don't own a candy or oil thermometer, simply sprinkle a pinch of flour into the oil. If it sizzles, it's ready.

Meanwhile, put the flour in a shallow dish. Dredge the clams in flour and set aside. Repeat with the oysters, keeping the clams and oysters separate.

When the oil is hot, using a slotted spoon or spider, fry one test clam to ensure your oil is at the correct temperature. If your test is successful and the clam is pale golden, using a slotted spoon or spider, lower half of the clams into the oil and fry for 45 seconds, then transfer to a plate or baking sheet lined with paper towels to drain. Sprinkle liberally with salt. Repeat the process with the remaining clams, letting the oil return to temperature before frying the next batch.

Next, fry half of the oysters. Using a slotted spoon or spider, lower half of the oysters into the oil and fry for 1 minute, then transfer to a plate or baking sheet lined with paper towels to drain. Sprinkle liberally with salt. Repeat the process with the remaining oysters, letting the oil return to temperature before frying the next batch.

Garnish the clams and oysters with fried sage leaves and serve with a dash of Tabasco, if desired.

SERVES 4 AS AN APPETIZER

2 quarts **canola**, **grapeseed**, or other **high-heat cooking oil**, for frying

½ cup **Wondra flour** or **all-purpose flour**

1 dozen **raw littleneck clams**, cleaned and shucked (see page 245)

1 dozen **raw oysters**, cleaned and shucked (see page 244)

Sea salt to taste

Quick-fried **sage leaves**, for garnish

Tabasco or other **hot sauce** to taste (optional)

FRIED FLOUNDER

SERVES 4

2 quarts **canola**, **grapeseed**, or other **high-heat cooking oil**, for frying

½ cup **Wondra flour** or **all-purpose flour**

4 (6- to 8-ounce) **skinless flounder fillets**

Sea salt and **freshly ground pepper** to taste

Tartar sauce, store-bought or homemade (page 241)

Suggested Side: Red Cabbage Slaw (page 222)

I opt not to fry anything too rich or with too much flavor—like sardines, for example. You could, but they wouldn't taste as good. On the other hand, light and flaky flounder has a delicate flavor that makes it a great choice for frying. It's no surprise that in England and Ireland, flounder or cod is usually the fish of choice for traditional fish & chips.

Pour the oil into a large pot, Dutch oven, or fryer. It should be at least 2 inches deep. Heat the oil to 375°F. If you don't own a candy or oil thermometer, simply sprinkle a pinch of flour into the oil. If it sizzles, it's ready.

Meanwhile, put the flour in a shallow dish. Rinse the fish and pat it dry with paper towel. Dredge the fish fillets in the flour, shaking off any excess.

When the oil is hot, using a slotted spoon or spider, gently slide the fish into the oil and fry for 1½ minutes, then transfer to a plate or baking sheet lined with paper towels to drain, frying in batches as necessary. Sprinkle liberally with salt and pepper. Serve with tartar sauce.

JOE
SAYS

—

As far as I'm concerned, squeezing lemon over cooked seafood does not enhance the flavor, but instead masks it. Maybe you need lemon if you're eating fish that's past its prime, but not with delicious fresh fish! If I want to taste lemon, I'll bite into one.

FULL-CIRCLE CRAB COMPANY

Columbia, North Carolina

FISHERMAN AND CRABBER WILLY PHILLIPS, from Columbia, North Carolina, is 100 percent committed to what he does. He sells wholesale and also has a full-service seafood retail shop, which offers a fresh haul to locals daily. Fishing is his livelihood and yet he and his wife, Feather, are multidimensional folks, living a Renaissance-type lifestyle—they are involved in the arts (Feather was one of the founders of the Pocosin Arts Folk School), build their own houses and boats, and are environmentally conscious among other interests.

TOSS WITH PASTA

SEA URCHIN
(**UNI**)

RECIPES

—

JOE
SAYS

Eat Pasta Uni with a
spoon so you can get
the sea urchin and pasta
together in one bite!

PASTA UNI

Uni *is the Japanese word* for sea urchin. Inside those prickly, porcupine-like spherical shells is something so sweet and creamy it actually tastes luxurious in your mouth. When the shells are cut open with scissors, inside is a five-pointed star safely tucked away. This meat of the sea urchin, which can range from bright yellow to orange, is normally considered a delicacy. In addition to being sold in the shell, uni is also packaged on small wooden trays with clear plastic lids. And there's no need to cook the buttery uni: just toss them with warm pasta and they nearly melt. My wife's eyes light up even at the mention of this dish.

In a large pot of salted, boiling water, cook the farfalle according to the package instructions until al dente. Drain the pasta and transfer to a large bowl. Drizzle with the olive oil and toss to combine.

Spoon the uni evenly over the cooked pasta, reserving a few, and toss to coat. Divide the pasta among four individual serving plates. Garnish each portion with a spoonful of the reserved uni. Serve immediately.

SERVES 4

Pinch of **sea salt**

1 pound **dried farfalle pasta**

1 tablespoon **extra-virgin olive oil**

6 ounces **uni**

ASK YOUR FISHMONGER

for freshly packaged uni (it usually comes on a wooden tray). If you're buying whole sea urchins, ask your fishmonger to open the sea urchin shells, remove the meat, and weigh it—you'll need 6 ounces.

SPAGHETTI VONGOLE

SERVES 4

4 pounds **raw New Zealand cockles** or **littleneck clams** (see Joe Says, page 121)

1 pound **dried spaghetti**

½ teaspoon **sea salt**

3 tablespoons **extra-virgin olive oil**

16 **garlic cloves**, minced

½ cup **dry white wine**

1 tablespoon chopped **flat-leaf parsley**

Red pepper flakes, for serving (optional)

There's a restaurant in Casa de Campo that I go to often. One day I ordered the *vongole* and after my first bite I knew: the *vongole* was made with butter! I felt like I was eating a stick of it because that's all I tasted—butter—not clams. Afterward I pulled the owner aside and told him he had taken the seafood flavor away from the dish by adding butter. I went back a week later and he said, "*No mantequilla, no mantequilla.*" So I guess he got the point. For me, *vongole* is supposed to be garlic, olive oil, clams, and white wine. That's it. Nothing else. If you're like me and like a little heat, add red pepper flakes to taste. I find it's a real crowd-pleaser.

Rinse the cockles or clams thoroughly, making sure no sand remains. Set aside.

Bring a large pot of water to a boil. Add the spaghetti and salt and cook according to the package instructions until al dente. Drain and set aside in a large serving bowl or pasta pot.

Meanwhile, coat the bottom of a large, heavy saucepan or Dutch oven with the olive oil. Add the garlic and heat the pan over low, stirring frequently, until the garlic just starts to turn golden, about 3 minutes. Add the cockles and wine and cover the pan. Steam until the shells open, about 8 minutes, discarding any that do not open. (You can continue to cook the unopened ones for a few more minutes because some may take a little longer.)

Gently spoon the open cockles in their shells and the cooking liquid over the pasta in the reserved bowl or pot. Add the parsley and gently toss until the pasta is thoroughly coated with the broth. Sprinkle with pepper flakes if desired. Divide the pasta between 4 shallow bowls and top with the cockles in their shells and a few spoonfuls of broth. Serve immediately.

" JOE SAYS

I use cockles in my *vongole* sauce because they're small and delicate and the shells look nice, sometimes with a slight greenish hue. You can substitute littlenecks if you can't find cockles.

LINGUINE BOTTARGA

Bottarga, often called a poor man's caviar, is fish roe from mullet or tuna that is dried and cured. A favorite of Sicilians, it is often shaved over pasta. The taste is so rich and savory, it's one that can win over even the most skeptical eaters. If you can't find whole bottarga, it's often available grated in a jar—ask your fishmonger.

In a large pot of salted boiling water, cook the linguine according to the package instructions until al dente. Drain the pasta and transfer to a large bowl. Drizzle with the olive oil and toss to combine.

Divide the pasta evenly between four plates. Using a fine microplane grater, cover the pasta with a light coating of bottarga, then toss lightly to coat. Use more if an intense flavor is desired. Serve immediately.

SERVES 4

Pinch of **sea salt**

1 pound **dried linguine**

¼ cup **extra-virgin olive oil**

4 ounces whole or grated **bottarga**

" JOE SAYS

Olive oil, yes! Cheese, hell no!

I HIDE THE CHEESE at my house when serving seafood pasta.

CUTTLEFISH INK PASTA

SERVES 4

Pinch of **sea salt**

1 pound **dried spaghetti**

2 tablespoons **extra-virgin olive oil**, divided, plus more for drizzling on the pasta

8 **garlic cloves**, finely minced, divided

2 tablespoons **cuttlefish ink**

½ pint **grape tomatoes**

½ pound **raw rock shrimp**

½ pound **raw sea scallops**, cut into quarters so they're the same size as the shrimp

Red pepper flakes, for serving

Cuttlefish is a cousin to calamari, and they both contain sacs of dark ink. You can buy readymade pasta that has this briny ink already mixed into the dough, but instead I like to tint regular spaghetti with a sauce that contains cuttlefish ink, which makes the pasta a dramatic black color and the flavor more intense. (It also stains your tongue, so beware!) We carry jarred cuttlefish ink at Citarella, and you can also find it online from specialty gourmet retailers. In addition to the ink, you're going to need two sauté pans for this recipe. All this may seem over the top, but the briny-tasting, garlicky black pasta topped with sweet shrimp and scallops is well worth it.

In a large pot of salted, boiling water, cook the spaghetti according to the package instructions until al dente. Drain the pasta and transfer to a large bowl. Drizzle with a few teaspoons of olive oil and toss to combine. Set aside.

Now you'll need two sauté pans, one small and one medium. Put 1 tablespoon oil in each pan and heat over low. Divide the garlic evenly between the two pans and stir to combine, cooking for a minute or two until it just starts to turn light golden. Turn the heat off under the medium sauté pan.

Next, add the ink to the small pan still on the heat. Heat the mixture, stirring occasionally, until warmed through, about 3 minutes. Then pour it over the cooked pasta and, using tongs, toss the pasta until it's evenly coated. Set aside.

Turn the heat back on under the medium pan and add the tomatoes and sauté over medium-high heat for 5 minutes, stirring constantly. Add the shrimp and scallops, increase the heat to high, and cook for 2 minutes, continuing to stir constantly, until the scallops brown ever so slightly.

Divide the ink-coated pasta among four plates or bowls and top with the sautéed shrimp, scallops, and tomatoes. Do not toss or the seafood will turn black. Finish with a sprinkle of red pepper flakes.

OUTERBANKS SEAFOOD

Nags Head, North Carolina

I'VE SPENT a major part of my life building the soft-shell crab business. Each crabber is important, so I've highlighted several of them throughout the book, like Robbie Beasley, a purveyor who I work with from Nags Head, North Carolina. He has been supplying me with beautiful crabs for years. He and his sister Marilyn have built a reputable company in the Outer Banks, a beach community where fishing boats line the shores and a strong coastal seafood heritage is present. I've been buying from Robbie and his sister for most of my career and I am proud to work with both of them.

CHILL
&
EAT RAW

LITTLENECK
CLAMS

RECIPES

—

HOW TO SERVE
RAW OYSTERS

Always shuck clams and oysters right before you're going to eat them for the freshest flavor. You can ask your fishmonger to do it for you, but just be sure to tell him or her NOT TO RINSE THEM! I knew a guy who asked a fishmonger to shuck two dozen oysters for him. When he got home and tasted them, the oysters had no flavor. An oyster without flavor? He called the store to talk with the guy who had shucked the oysters. The fishmonger said, "I was doing you a favor, Mister—I rinsed them twice!" Enough said.

I recommend about six oysters per person as an appetizer. Serve on a bed of seaweed or over crushed ice (see page 179).

" JOE SAYS

If you're going to shuck oysters or clams (see pages 244–245), you're going to need an oyster or clam knife, respectively. If you use a kitchen knife you're going to hurt yourself.

HELLO!?

Mignonette sauce? How do you taste the oyster if you put vinegar on it?

HOW TO SERVE
RAW CLAMS

Serve raw clams on the half shell on a bed of crushed ice or seaweed so they don't roll off the serving plate. See page 245 for how to shuck clams, or you can ask your fishmonger to do the work and save the shells for you. I recommend about six clams per person for an appetizer serving.

HELLO!? At parties I see people put cocktail sauce on raw clams. Hello? **WHAT ARE YOU TASTING?** Not the clam, that's for sure.

DIY CRUSHED ICE

Crushed ice is crucial for a classic raw seafood presentation because the clam or oyster is going to roll off ice cubes. If you don't have a crushed-ice maker in your freezer, fill resealable freezer bags halfway with ice and crush it with a heavy skillet, rolling pin, or wooden mallet. Be sure you choose a sturdy, unbreakable surface to work on. Try not to puncture the bag. You can put the ice back in the freezer until you're ready to use it.

HOW TO SERVE
STONE CRAB CLAWS

ASK YOUR
FISHMONGER

*for ½ to ¾ pound of
whole stone crab claws
per person.*

I'll be honest. Stone crab claws are work. But the only things you need in order to eat them are a hammer or mallet and your mouth. Those metal crab crackers that look like nutcrackers won't do; they're not strong enough to crack the hard shell. Just give the bright orange cooked claws a quick whack and pull out the delicate meat. Don't hit them too hard or you'll get too many pieces of shell. Because they always come cooked, you just crack 'em and eat 'em. Serve the meat with a little mustard sauce if you like, which you can buy prepared or make by simply whisking together ¼ cup Dijon mustard, 3 tablespoons mayonnaise, 1 teaspoon white wine, 2 teaspoons lemon juice, and ⅛ teaspoon sea salt.

" JOE SAYS

Florida stone crab claws always come cooked and are available mid-October through mid-May.

Lobster and crab can only be sold three ways—live, cooked, or frozen—because, unlike fish and other seafood, they spoil very quickly.

OYSTER SHOOTERS

Seafood seasoning salt

4 ounces premium ice-cold **vodka**

4 shucked **raw oysters**, any type

Tabasco sauce

ASK YOUR FISHMONGER

to shuck the oysters for you.

Cocktail and appetizer in one! A briny oyster dropped in a shot of vodka is a pretty perfect combo in my book. Chill the shot glasses for a cool presentation, literally.

Pour a small amount of seafood seasoning into a small bowl. Dampen the rims of four chilled shot glasses with a wet paper towel and dip the rims into the seasoning.

Divide the cold vodka between the four prepared glasses and drop one oyster into each one. Top with a dash of Tabasco and serve immediately.

" JOE SAYS

Times have changed. Don't believe that you should only eat oysters in the months that contain an "R" (September through April), which originates back to a time when harvesting wasn't regulated, and warm summer water temperatures could affect the oysters. Today, oysters harvested legally are safe to eat year-round.

JOE'S CEVICHE

In ceviche, you let your limes do the "cooking." Raw seafood gets a pop of flavor from citrus and jalapeño peppers here, and the citric acid of the lime juice "cooks" the fish, turning it from translucent to opaque, just like heat does. The fish also firms up some, as if it's been cooked with heat. I cut the seafood into the same-size pieces so it marinates at the same rate, and it makes it look like a professional made it too!

In a large bowl, combine the scallops, shrimp, fluke, tomatoes, onion, and jalapeños, to taste, and toss to combine. Sprinkle with a few generous pinches of salt and the cilantro and toss again. Pour the lime juice over the mixture, making sure the mixture is completely covered by the liquid. Cover with plastic wrap and let sit at room temperature for at least 1 hour. Use a slotted spoon to serve as is or over white rice. Garnish with avocado.

SERVES 6 AS AN APPETIZER

½ pound **raw sea scallops**, cut into ½-inch pieces

½ pound **raw large shrimp** (16 to 20 per pound), peeled, deveined (see page 246), and cut into ½-inch pieces

½ pound **skinless fluke** or **skinless striped bass fillet**, cut into ½-inch pieces

2 **plum tomatoes**, seeded and pulp discarded, cut into ¼-inch dice (about ½ cup)

1 small **yellow onion**, cut into ¼-inch dice

1 to 2 **jalapeño peppers**, seeded and finely chopped

Sea salt to taste

½ cup roughly chopped **cilantro** leaves

1½ cups freshly squeezed **lime juice** (from about 10 limes), plus more as needed

White rice, for serving (optional)

2 ripe **avocados**, peeled, pitted, and sliced, for garnish

PECONIC PRIDE

Water Mill, New York

HOWARD PICKERELL, owner of Peconic Pride, grows oysters in the pristine waters of Long Island's Peconic Bay. Howard and I have both been in business a long time, yet we've only started working together in recent years—I'm always on the lookout for new suppliers of quality seafood. Going out on Howard's boat, I saw the process of how he farms oysters year-round with great dedication and commitment. The healthy ecosystem of the bay creates beautiful oysters.

RAW FISH
ITALIAN-STYLE

If you've reached the crudo stage, this is a milestone in fish appreciation. Crudo is the Italian version of sashimi—sliced raw fish—but instead of soy and wasabi, other, more Italian-style ingredients are used to complement the fish. This is one of my favorite ways to start a meal. When you serve this, it looks like you know what you are doing!

All of my crudos involve some kind of sea salt and high-quality extra-virgin olive oil as a foundation. I add subtle flavors, like a touch of citrus or a handful of herbs. Take notice and compare the flavors and textures of the fish like you would fine wines.

Crudos require a really good knife in order to slice the fish properly, which is against the grain (just like when you slice beef). Once we have that understanding, the hard part is done.

I've not only chosen fish with the best textures to eat raw, but also ones that are readily available, not hard-to-find fish like those you see in high-end sushi restaurants, such as Japanese mackerel (saba), bonito (katsu), or hamachi (yellowtail).

BRANZINO

THE MYTH OF
"SUSHI GRADE"

THERE'S LOTS OF CONFUSION surrounding the term "sushi grade." Let me clarify it for you.

"Sushi grade" equals freshness. That's it. And despite what many think, there are no official regulations determining what level of freshness designates "sushi-grade" quality.

Many stores use this term because of the inconsistency of their seafood products. Now, keep in mind, sushi-grade fish can have different degrees of freshness. On a freshness scale from 1 to 10, Citarella's fish would be a 9 or 10 (10 being the best), while other stores' fish might just be a 7 or below. I can confidently say that everything at Citarella is sushi grade because it's always fresh.

We buy the highest-quality fish possible at all times. If we don't like what we see in the fish market that day, we do without it. That is one of the ways we have made our reputation.

At Citarella, I'll eat almost anything raw, from tuna and salmon to scallops and fluke. Buy your fish from a reputable purveyor who sells only fresh seafood, and you can do the same.

TUNA CRUDO

There really are only good things to say about the combination of fresh raw tuna, olive oil, and salt. There's no better way to taste fish!

Using a very sharp knife, slice the chilled tuna against the grain into ¼-inch-thick slices. Lay the slices on a chilled serving plate in an overlapping pattern.

Drizzle the tuna with the oil and sprinkle with salt. Serve immediately.

SERVES 2 AS AN APPETIZER

8 ounces **center-cut ahi tuna fillet**, chilled

1 tablespoon **extra-virgin olive oil**

Black Hawaiian sea salt or **French grey salt** to taste

BRANZINO
CRUDO

SERVES 2 AS AN APPETIZER

8 ounces **skinless branzino** fillet, chilled

1 tablespoon **extra-virgin olive oil**

Pink Hawaiian sea salt to taste

1 teaspoon chopped **chives**

I've never seen branzino crudo done anywhere else, but I decided to try it with this particular fish because of its sweet taste and tender texture. It worked wonderfully and now it's a favorite.

Using a very sharp knife, slice the chilled branzino against the grain into ¼-inch-thick slices. Lay the slices on a chilled serving plate.

Drizzle with the olive oil. Sprinkle with salt and the chives just before serving.

SCALLOP CRUDO

It was New Year's Day in Denmark, and I was at a Michelin-star restaurant. An excellent scallop crudo was part of the meal. In true Scandinavian style, the presentation was stark and minimalist, which made it all the more deceptively delicious. The silky, sweet texture of the raw scallop combined with the subtle clementine juice and crunch of sea salt and spicy radish was so special that I knew I was going to have to recreate the dish at home. It was a good start to the year if you ask me.

Using a very sharp knife, slice the scallops crosswise against the grain into ¼-inch-thick slices. Arrange them on a chilled platter.

Garnish with the radish matchsticks and drizzle with the olive oil and clementine juice. Sprinkle with salt and serve immediately.

SERVES 2 AS AN APPETIZER

3 **raw sea scallops**, chilled

1 **red radish**, cut into thin matchsticks

2 tablespoons **extra-virgin olive oil**

2 tablespoons freshly squeezed **clementine juice**

Black Hawaiian sea salt to taste

" JOE SAYS

Keep the scallops cold until right before slicing them for crudo, as it makes them easier to cut.

SALMON
CRUDO

SERVES 2 AS AN APPETIZER

1 large **seedless cucumber**, ends trimmed

8 ounces **skinless Norwegian salmon fillet**, chilled

1 tablespoon **extra-virgin olive oil**

Sea salt to taste

Microgreens, for garnish

Cucumber and salmon are a natural pairing because the crisp texture of the cuke complements the rich, fatty fish. A handful of fresh microgreens adds a little artistry to the plate. It's the small details that make a difference in presentation.

Slice the cucumber in half lengthwise and scrape out the seeds using a spoon. Use a chef's knife to cut each half into long, thin vertical planks. Stack the planks and cut them into 2-inch pieces.

Lay the cucumber pieces in a single layer on a serving platter and cover with a damp paper towel. Refrigerate while you prepare the crudo.

Using a very sharp knife, slice the fish against the grain into ¼-inch-thick slices. Lay a slice of crudo on a cucumber slice and gently fold the fish onto itself. Drizzle the salmon with the olive oil and finish with a sprinkle of salt. Garnish with microgreens and serve.

FLUKE CRUDO

8 ounces **skinless fluke fillet**, chilled

1 cup store-bought **seaweed salad**

1 tablespoon **extra-virgin olive oil**

Hawaiian red sea salt to taste

The unique, almost noodle-like texture of seaweed salad adds to the mild, tender texture of the fluke here. A pinch of bright red Hawaiian sea salt, which gets its color from volcanic red clay, is supposed to have healing properties. I just use it because it tastes—and looks—great!

Using a very sharp knife, slice the chilled fluke against the grain into ¼-inch-thick slices.

Arrange small mounds of seaweed salad—as many mounds as you have pieces of fish—on a chilled serving plate. Gently lay a folded slice of fish on each mound. Drizzle with the oil and sprinkle with red sea salt. Serve immediately.

TARTARE

Tartare means "raw and chopped" and is known historically as a beef preparation that combines raw meat with egg, capers, and other seasonings. Fish and seafood versions of tartare are now equally popular, if not more so. Tartares require a couple more ingredients than crudos, as tartares are about the combination of flavors and textures. You'll also find tartares chopped into many different sizes, some fine and some chunkier. There is no right or wrong, as long as the fish is fresh (WHAT A SURPRISE!).

I'm not trying to be redundant using the same fish for the tartares that I use for the crudos, but these are the textures that work best for raw recipes—and are the easiest to find.

BRANZINO TARTARE

SERVES 4 AS AN
APPETIZER

16 ounces **skinless branzino fillet,** chilled

¼ cup freshly squeezed **orange juice**

2 teaspoons chopped **basil**

2 teaspoons **extra-virgin olive oil**, plus more for serving

Sea salt to taste

Toasted **Tuscan bread**, for serving

ASK YOUR
FISHMONGER

to remove the skin from the fillet, as eating it raw will not be appetizing.

I like to think of this as a pure "Joe creation." A Mediterranean staple, this lean fish is extremely tender—and one of my favorites. I like to enhance the naturally delicate flavor with basil and orange juice.

Using a very sharp knife, cut the branzino into ½-inch cubes. Do not overchop or the fish will turn mushy.

In a medium bowl, combine the fish, orange juice, basil, and oil and gently toss to coat. Add a sprinkle or two of salt to taste. Divide the tartare between four (4-ounce) ramekins and gently press down on the mixture to form to the mold. (If you don't have 4-ounce ramekins, you can use a ½ cup measure as a mold.) Invert each ramekin onto an individual serving plate. Drizzle lightly with olive oil. Serve with toasted bread.

SALMON TARTARE

A dash of salty soy sauce and acidic lime balances out the fatty richness of the salmon. Ginger and wasabi add a little kick too. I like this dish as an appetizer, but you can also double the quantities and serve it for a light summer lunch—or as a topping on a poke bowl.

Using a very sharp knife, cut the salmon into ½-inch cubes. Do not overchop or the texture will turn mushy.

In a medium bowl, whisk together the lime juice, soy sauce, sesame oil, wasabi paste, and grated ginger until well combined and the paste is completely dissolved. Add the salmon and stir to combine.

To serve, divide the seaweed salad between two plates. Spoon half of the salmon mixture into a 4-ounce ramekin and invert it onto the seaweed salad. (If you don't have a 4-ounce ramekin, you can use a ½ cup measure as a mold.) Repeat with the remaining tartare. Garnish with additional freshly grated ginger if you like.

SERVES 2 AS AN APPETIZER

8 ounces **skinless salmon fillet,** chilled

Juice of ½ **lime**

1½ teaspoons **soy sauce**

½ teaspoon **sesame oil**

¼ teaspoon **wasabi paste**

¼ teaspoon freshly grated **ginger,** plus more for garnish if desired

1 cup store-bought **seaweed salad**

TUNA TARTARE

SERVES 4 AS AN
APPETIZER

16 ounces **center-cut ahi tuna fillet**, chilled

2 teaspoons **extra-virgin olive oil**

Sea salt to taste

3 teaspoons chopped **cilantro** leaves, divided, plus more for garnish

1 ripe **avocado**

1 **mango**, peeled and cut into ¼-inch pieces

2 teaspoons freshly squeezed **lime juice**

Toasted **baguette**, for serving

Tuna is most likely what comes to mind when people think of fish tartares, as it was one of the original takes on the well-known beef preparation. Although tuna tartare is everywhere, I could not leave this classic out of the book.

Using a very sharp knife, cut the fish into ¾-inch cubes. Do not overchop or the texture will turn mushy. Drizzle with the oil and sprinkle with a few pinches of salt and 1 teaspoon cilantro. Gently toss to coat. Refrigerate until ready to serve.

Halve and pit the avocado. Scoop out the flesh with a spoon and place in a mixing bowl. Smash the avocado with a fork until smooth. Add the mango, remaining cilantro, and lime juice to the bowl and stir to combine. Add salt to taste.

Divide the avocado-mango mixture between four chilled serving plates, arranging it into a mound. Top with the tuna and finish with a sprinkle of cilantro and salt, if desired. Serve with slices of toasted baguette.

FLUKE TARTARE

Fluke sashimi is very common, so I decided to use the fish in a tartare. The texture is much more delicate than tuna or salmon, which is especially noticeable when eating it raw. I added cucumber and grapefruit juice for a refreshing twist.

Using a very sharp knife, cut the fluke into ½-inch cubes. Do not overchop or the texture will turn mushy.

In a medium bowl, combine the fluke, diced cucumber, grapefruit juice, and olive oil. Gently toss to coat. Season with salt and pepper to taste and toss again. Divide the cucumber slices between four serving plates and arrange them in a lattice pattern. Divide the tartare among the four plates and garnish with grapefruit if desired. Serve with pieces of flatbread.

SERVES 4 AS AN
APPETIZER

16 ounces **skinless fluke fillet**, chilled

½ **seedless cucumber**, cut into small dice

3 tablespoons freshly squeezed **grapefruit juice**

1 tablespoon **extra-virgin olive oil**

French grey salt and **freshly ground rainbow peppercorns** to taste

Thin **cucumber slices**, vertically cut, for serving

Segments from ½ **grapefruit**, diced, for garnish (optional)

4 pieces **flatbread**, for serving

SPANISH MACKEREL TARTARE

SERVES 2 AS AN APPETIZER

8 ounces skinless **Spanish mackerel fillet**, chilled

1 tablespoon chopped **chives**

1 tablespoon **extra-virgin olive oil**

Sea salt or **French grey sea salt** to taste

Microgreens, for garnish

Toasted Italian bread, for serving

This hearty fish has a full flavor and is definitely one for people who love the taste of fish. I like to serve this bold-tasting tartare on toast for crunch and balance.

Using a very sharp knife, cut the mackerel into ½-inch cubes. Do not overchop or the texture will turn mushy.

In a chilled medium bowl, combine the fish, chives, and olive oil and toss gently to coat. Season with salt to taste. Serve chilled with microgreens and slices of toasted bread.

SAVORY

SIDES

RECIPES

—

GRILLED ASPARAGUS

SERVES 4

1 pound **asparagus,**
ends removed (see
Joe Says, below)

1 to 2 tablespoons
**extra-virgin olive
oil**

Sea salt and
**freshly ground
pepper** to taste

" JOE SAYS
—

The simplest way to
remove the ends of
fresh asparagus is to
bend each spear at
the bottom until it
snaps. The asparagus
will naturally break at
the point where the
tender stalk meets
the fibrous stem.

Grilling asparagus brings out its natural sweetness. In the summer I like
to throw a pound on the grill alongside whole fish like porgy (page 44) or
branzino (page 40).

Preheat your stovetop grill pan or outdoor grill. Put the asparagus in
a large bowl, along with enough olive oil to coat. Season with salt and
pepper and toss well.

Cook the asparagus on the preheated grill until lightly charred, 4 to 6
minutes total, turning them several times, depending on the thickness of
the spears. Serve immediately or at room temperature.

SAUTÉED BROCCOLI RABE

A classic Italian side dish, broccoli rabe has a strong flavor—it's almost an acquired taste. My wife and daughter didn't eat it for years, but now they do, so don't give up if your family doesn't take to it on the first go. It's a good complement to meaty Seared Tuna Steaks (page 30).

In a large saucepan, heat the olive oil and garlic over medium heat, stirring the garlic until it just starts to turn golden, about 2 minutes.

Add the broccoli rabe and cover the pan. Cook for 4 to 5 minutes, or until the desired texture is achieved. I like mine al dente. If you like yours softer, cook a few minutes more.

Sprinkle with red pepper flakes and serve.

SERVES 4

3 tablespoons **extra-virgin olive oil**

4 **garlic cloves**, finely chopped

1 bunch **broccoli rabe**, ends trimmed

Red pepper flakes to taste

TOMATO & BASIL
BRUSCHETTA

SERVES 4

2 pounds heirloom **tomatoes**, finely chopped

4 **garlic cloves**, finely minced

6 **basil** leaves, chopped

5 tablespoons **extra-virgin olive oil**, divided

Sea salt and **freshly ground pepper** to taste

1 **baguette**, sliced into ½-inch-thick slices

" JOE SAYS

Try heating the tomato topping to serve over pasta or your favorite fish.

An Italian classic, bruschetta (pronounced brus-ketta) is fresh and fast. Need I even say, the riper the tomatoes, the better the flavor here. I like serving these toasts as an appetizer before grilled fish. I also spoon the topping over mild fish like Poached Wild Striped Bass (page 124) for an easy summer dinner.

Preheat the oven to 375°F.

In a large bowl, combine the tomatoes, garlic, and basil. Drizzle with 3 tablespoons of the olive oil and season with a few pinches of salt and pepper and toss to combine. Set aside at room temperature.

Place the baguette slices on a rimmed baking sheet and, using a pastry brush and the remaining olive oil, lightly coat each piece with a thin layer of oil. Toast the baguette slices for 5 to 8 minutes, or until they just start to turn golden brown on the edges. Remove the toasts from the oven and transfer to a serving platter. Top each slice with a spoonful of the tomato mixture. Serve immediately.

SAUTÉED
BRUSSELS SPROUTS
& MUSHROOMS

I peel the leaves from each sprout for this dish, and this takes a little patience. If you know me, patience is not my specialty. It's worth it though: when you sauté them, they wilt and become sweet and tender. Don't make this dish for an army, as it'll take too long. But you won't regret the effort if you keep it to just a few lucky guests. This is the perfect side to serve with Seasonal Boned Shad (page 89).

Peel the individual leaves off of each sprout; discard the centers of the sprouts.

Heat 2 tablespoons of the olive oil in a large sauté pan over medium-high heat. Add the Brussels sprout leaves and cook for 2 to 3 minutes, or until they start to soften. Remove them from the pan and set aside in a large serving bowl.

Add the remaining oil to the pan and heat over medium heat. Add the mushrooms and sauté for 2 to 3 minutes, or until slightly softened or the desired texture is achieved.

Transfer the mushrooms to the serving bowl with the leaves and toss to combine. Season the mixture to taste with salt and pepper and sprinkle with the balsamic vinegar. Toss to coat. Serve immediately or at room temperature.

SERVES 4

1 pound **Brussels sprouts**, trimmed

4 tablespoons **extra-virgin olive oil**, divided

8 ounces **mushrooms** (such as oyster, white, shiitake, or quartered portobello), sliced

Sea salt and **freshly ground pepper** to taste

2 tablespoons **aged balsamic vinegar**

RED CABBAGE SLAW

SERVES 4 TO 6

¼ cup **distilled white vinegar**

1 teaspoon **cane sugar**

1 teaspoon **sea salt**

¼ cup **extra-virgin olive oil**

1 medium **red cabbage** (about 1¼ pounds), cored and very thinly sliced (about 6 cups)

Freshly ground pepper to taste

This vinegar-based slaw cuts the fat of deep-fried foods, and is especially delicious served alongside Fried Flounder (page 154). You can personalize this very basic recipe with your own favorite flavors. Add a tablespoon or two of mustard, pickle juice, and/or mayonnaise to the dressing before tossing with the cabbage. You know me though: I like it just like this—nice and simple!

In a large bowl, combine the vinegar, sugar, and salt. Whisk until the sugar and salt dissolves.

Add the olive oil and whisk until combined. Put the cabbage in the bowl and toss until fully coated with the dressing. Season with pepper to taste. Let stand at room temperature for 30 minutes before serving.

CAULIFLOWER PURÉE

While mashed potatoes may be more popular, puréed cauliflower has gained traction and is a nice change because it's slightly lighter and even more elegant. Its creamy texture pairs especially well with Seared Sea Scallops (page 98). Don't be shy with the sea salt, because cauliflower tends to be mild and sweet and tastes better with a good dash.

In a medium saucepan over high heat, combine the cauliflower, garlic, onion, broth, salt, and pepper. Bring to a boil, cover, then lower the heat and simmer for about 10 minutes, or until the cauliflower is tender.

Carefully transfer the contents of the pot into a blender and add the cream and butter. Purée the mixture on low until smooth.

Serve immediately, or refrigerate and reheat in a saucepan just before serving.

SERVES 4

1 medium **cauliflower**, cut into florets

1 **garlic clove**, peeled

½ cup coarsely chopped **white onion**

½ cup **chicken broth**

1 tablespoon **sea salt**

¼ teaspoon **freshly ground white pepper**

3 tablespoons **heavy cream**

3 tablespoons **unsalted butter**, at room temperature

ROASTED CAULIFLOWER

SERVES 4

1 medium
cauliflower, cut into
florets

3 tablespoons **extra-
virgin olive oil**

Sea salt and
**freshly ground
pepper** to taste

Leaves from
two sprigs fresh
rosemary

Make sure your oven is hot before you start cooking the cauliflower, and you'll get tender, caramelized sweet florets every time. Serve this satisfying side dish with Broiled Fluke with Herbes de Provence (page 86).

Preheat the oven to 375°F.

Put the cauliflower on a rimmed baking sheet, drizzle with the oil, and season with salt and pepper. Using your hands, toss the cauliflower until it's thoroughly coated. Arrange the cauliflower in a single layer on the pan and bake for 25 minutes, or until the florets turn golden brown and are tender when pierced with a fork.

Sprinkle with the rosemary leaves and serve.

CORN & EDAMAME
SALAD

I like to make this side in the summer when corn is at its best. The crunch of the edamame complements the sweet, tender corn, and the colors make any dish pop. The combination pairs extremely well with grilled seafood, especially thick salmon fillets right off the grill (page 37).

Heat the olive oil in a medium sauté pan over medium heat. Add the corn and cook for 1 to 2 minutes. Add the edamame and continue to cook until it's just warmed through.

Season the mixture with salt and pepper to taste and serve immediately or at room temperature.

SERVES 4

2 tablespoons **extra-virgin olive oil**

4 ears **corn**, shucked and kernels cut off the cob

8 ounces shelled **edamame** (2 cups), thawed if frozen

Sea salt and **freshly ground pepper** to taste

SAUTÉED CORN & TOMATO SALAD

SERVES 4

1 tablespoon **extra-virgin olive oil**

3 ears **corn,** shucked and kernels cut off the cob

1 pint **cherry** or **grape tomatoes**, halved

Sea salt and **freshly ground pepper** to taste

Top this classic combination with freshly steamed lobster meat (page 127), and you've suddenly got an elegant meal. This salad also goes nicely with Broiled Florida Red Snapper (page 80). Combining this summer produce adds bright, sweet flavors to almost any plate.

Heat the olive oil in a medium sauté pan over low heat. Add the corn and sauté for 3 minutes, or until slightly softened. Transfer the corn to a bowl and allow it to cool for a few minutes. Stir in the tomatoes and sprinkle with a few pinches of salt and pepper to taste. Toss to combine and serve.

ROASTED FENNEL

Cooked fennel, with its slight anise flavor, is a classic side to seafood, like Sautéed Wild Striped Bass Fillets (page 111). Searing the bulbs on the stovetop after baking them gives them a slight golden caramelization, making them sweet.

SERVES 4

2 bulbs **fennel,** trimmed

4 teaspoons **extra-virgin olive oil**

Sea salt and **freshly ground pepper** to taste

Preheat the oven to 375°F.

Slice the fennel bulbs lengthwise into ½-inch-thick slices. Brush the slices lightly on both sides with olive oil and season with salt and pepper. Arrange them in a single layer on a rimmed baking sheet. Roast the fennel for 30 minutes, or until it is fork-tender.

When the fennel is finished cooking, heat a large sauté pan on the stovetop over medium-high. When the pan is hot (you can test it with a drop of water; if it sizzles it's ready), sear the fennel for 2 minutes per side, or until the slices turn golden brown. Serve immediately. (They also taste great at room temperature.)

LENTIL SALAD

SERVES 4

1 cup **dried brown lentils**

1 large **carrot**, peeled

½ medium **onion**, finely diced (about ½ cup)

10 to 12 **green beans**, trimmed and cut into ¼-inch pieces

1 tablespoon **extra-virgin olive oil**

1 teaspoon **balsamic vinegar**

¼ teaspoon **sea salt**

Freshly ground pepper to taste

This salad is light yet extremely satisfying. Pair it with a creamy-tasting fish like Steamed Florida Grouper (page 123), and dinner is done.

Using a fine-mesh strainer, rinse the lentils, then put them in a small pot and cover with 2 inches of water. Bring to a boil over high heat, then lower the heat and simmer for about 30 minutes, or until the lentils are tender. When the lentils are finished cooking, drain any excess water from the pot and put them in a medium serving bowl.

Meanwhile, shave the carrot with a vegetable peeler into thin strips, then cut the strips into ½-inch pieces (you should get about ¾ cup).

Add the carrot, onion, and green beans to the lentils and gently toss to combine.

Sprinkle with the olive oil, vinegar, salt, and pepper and toss again until everything is well mixed. Serve immediately or store in the refrigerator for up to 2 days.

SAUTÉED MIXED MUSHROOMS

Earthy and flavorful, sautéed mushrooms are a great addition to any fish dish. Because they are hearty and meaty themselves, they pair especially well with swordfish, but consider serving them on their own as an antipasto course alongside Insalata di Mare (page 134) and Crispy Calamari (page 146).

Heat the olive oil in a large sauté pan over medium-high heat. When warm, add the mushrooms and sauté for 6 to 8 minutes, stirring occasionally. When the mushrooms are slightly softened, season to taste with salt and pepper and top with the rosemary.

SERVES 4

¼ cup **extra-virgin olive oil**

1 pound **mixed mushrooms** (such as portobello, shiitake, and oyster), thinly sliced

Sea salt and **freshly ground pepper** to taste

2 teaspoons minced fresh **rosemary**

CHUNKY
MASHED POTATOES

2 pounds **Idaho potatoes**, peeled and cut into 2-inch chunks

½ teaspoon **sea salt**, plus more as needed

¼ cup **whole milk**

8 tablespoons (1 stick) **unsalted butter**, melted

Freshly ground pepper to taste

On a trip to Sicily I was surprised by a twist on mashed potatoes: capers and lemon juice stirred right in. Wow, was it delicious (see page 132). Here, I'm sharing the classic version I whip up when I'm craving something comforting.

Put the potatoes and ½ teaspoon salt in a medium pot and cover with cold water. Bring to a boil over high heat, then reduce to a simmer, cooking for 20 minutes, or until the potatoes are tender when pierced with a fork.

Drain the cooked potatoes and return them to the pot. Add the milk and butter and mash with a fork to the desired texture. Stir in salt and pepper to taste.

CRISPY STOVETOP
NEW POTATOES

These guys are a home run. When you're choosing potatoes for this recipe, look for the smallest available. You want about 2-inch pieces after they're halved or quartered, which are small enough to crisp up nice and golden brown. I especially love these with Roasted Fluke (page 68).

In a large sauté pan over low, heat the olive oil and garlic. Cook, stirring occasionally, until the garlic starts to turn golden, about 1 to 2 minutes.

Add the potatoes to the pan and cook until the cut side is crisp and brown and the inside is fork-tender, about 35 minutes, stirring every 5 to 8 minutes. Season with salt and pepper to taste. Sprinkle with the rosemary and toss to combine. Serve immediately.

SERVES 4

¼ cup **extra-virgin olive oil**

2 **garlic cloves**, minced

1 pound **baby potatoes**, halved (or quartered depending on their size, see headnote)

Sea salt and **freshly ground pepper** to taste

1 tablespoon finely chopped fresh **rosemary**

MASHED
SWEET POTATOES

SERVES 4

2 pounds
sweet potatoes,
peeled and cut into
2-inch chunks

Pinch of **sea salt**

4 tablespoons
unsalted butter,
at room temperature

1 teaspoon freshly
squeezed **orange
juice**

⅛ teaspoon ground
cinnamon

Sea salt and
**freshly ground
pepper** to taste

The cinnamon and orange juice in this sweet potato mash are optional. Spiced up, this colorful side pairs nicely with simple seafood like Sautéed Nantucket Bay Scallops (page 101); if plain, you can serve this naturally sweet mashed root vegetable with most anything.

Put the potatoes and salt in a medium pot and cover with cold water by at least 1 inch. Bring to a boil over high heat, then reduce to a simmer and cook for 20 minutes, or until the potatoes are tender when pierced with a fork.

Drain the cooked potatoes and return them to the pot. Add the butter, orange juice, and cinnamon and mash with a fork to the desired texture. Stir in salt and pepper to taste. Serve immediately.

POTATO PURÉE

Being a big fan of olive oil myself, you'll find very little butter in this book, but here is where I use butter. And boy does this recipe have lots of it. Just a quick turn in the food mill (or food processor if you don't have a food mill), and you've got potatoes everyone will love—they're velvety smooth and downright decadent. Serve them alongside Sautéed Skate (page 107), and it'll feel like a bistro meal.

Put the potatoes and a few large pinches salt in a medium pot and cover with cold water by at least 1 inch. Bring to a boil over high heat, then reduce to a simmer and cook for 20 minutes, or until the potatoes are tender when pierced with a fork.

Drain the cooked potatoes and turn them through a food mill using the medium grind plate. Stir in the milk, butter, and salt to taste until smooth and creamy. Alternatively, put the drained potatoes in the food processor with the milk, butter, and salt to taste and pulse several times until just smooth, about 15 to 20 seconds. You don't want to overprocess the potatoes, or they'll turn gummy. Serve immediately.

SERVES 4

2 pounds **Yukon gold potatoes** (about 6 large), peeled and cut into 2-inch chunks

Sea salt to taste

1 cup **whole milk**

12 tablespoons **unsalted butter**, at room temperature

" JOE SAYS

This recipe requires more salt than others. You'll need 2 to 3 teaspoons to achieve the right taste here. You'll taste how the flavor just becomes richer and better!

TOMATO & RED ONION
SALAD

SERVES 4

2 pounds ripe
heirloom tomatoes,
cut into 1½-inch
chunks

1 medium **red onion**,
peeled and thinly
sliced

¼ cup **extra-virgin
olive oil**

Sea salt and
**freshly ground
pepper** to taste

❝
JOE
SAYS
—

Never put tomatoes
in the fridge—always
store them at room
temperature and you'll
get the best taste.

The longer this salad sits, the more it marinates and creates a delicious tomato juice that, after the salad is gone, I like to reserve and toss with pasta. This salad also pairs well with Local Bluefish on the Grill (page 38).

In a medium bowl, combine the tomatoes and onions. Drizzle with the olive oil and sprinkle with salt and pepper to taste. Gently toss to coat. Cover and allow to marinate at room temperature for 2 to 3 hours. Serve using a slotted spoon.

SAUTÉED GREEN BEANS

Sautéed garlic and olive oil coats the green beans here, making a super-simple side dish extra special. Pair these fresh beans with Oven-Roasted Montauk Tilefish (page 64).

Put ½ inch of water into a large sauté pan and bring it to a boil. Add the beans and cover the pan. Steam the beans for 5 minutes, or to the desired tenderness. Drain the beans and put them in a serving bowl.

In the same pan, heat the olive oil and garlic over low heat. As soon as the garlic starts to turn golden, about 3 minutes, remove the pan from the heat and pour the garlic oil over the steamed green beans. Season to taste with salt and pepper.

Serve immediately or at room temperature.

SERVES 4

1 pound
green beans,
trimmed

¼ cup **extra-virgin
olive oil**

4 **garlic cloves**,
thinly sliced

Sea salt and
**freshly ground
pepper** to taste

SAUTÉED SPINACH

SERVES 4

2 **garlic cloves**, finely chopped

2 tablespoons **extra-virgin olive oil**

2 bunches fresh **baby spinach** leaves, washed

Sea salt and **freshly ground pepper** to taste

"

JOE
SAYS

—

Sauté spinach quickly, as if you're cooking it rare, because if you overcook it, it becomes mushy.

With the popularity of kale, people seem to have forgotten about spinach. But I haven't. A light sauté and the leaves become so tender they almost melt in your mouth. A favorite like this goes well with Poached Salmon (page 116).

Put the garlic and olive oil in a large sauté pan and cook slowly over low heat, until the garlic just starts to turn golden, about 3 to 5 minutes.

Add the spinach, stir, and cover the pan. Let the greens wilt for about 3 minutes, or to the desired texture. Season to taste with salt and pepper and serve.

GRILLED ZUCCHINI

Don't buy huge zucchini—they can be spongy and flavorless. Look for the small, delicate ones that are sweet and tender. A quick sear keeps them from getting mushy or falling apart. Whenever I'm grilling, I like to throw a couple of these versatile summer vegetables on the grates for a quick side.

Preheat your stovetop grill pan or outdoor grill to medium-high heat. Put the zucchini in a large bowl and drizzle with the olive oil. Add a few pinches of salt and pepper and toss to coat.

Cook the zucchini on the preheated grill for 2 minutes per side, or until the strips get grill marks and just become tender. Serve immediately or at room temperature.

SERVES 4

4 **zucchini,** trimmed and cut lengthwise into ¼-inch-thick strips

2 tablespoons **extra-virgin olive oil**

Sea salt and **freshly ground pepper** to taste

CLASSIC
SEAFOOD
SAUCES

CITARELLA
FISH
COUNTER

SPICY COCKTAIL SAUCE

MAKES ABOUT 1½ CUPS

1 (12-ounce) bottle **chili sauce**

¼ cup **ketchup**

1 tablespoon freshly squeezed **lemon juice**

2 teaspoons **distilled white vinegar**

2 tablespoons finely grated fresh **horseradish** root or prepared horseradish, or more to taste

1 teaspoon **Worcestershire sauce**

½ teaspoon **cane sugar**, or more to taste

Sea salt to taste

Dash of **Tabasco** sauce

Put all the ingredients in a medium bowl and stir well to combine. Salt to taste. Add more horseradish, sugar, or salt as desired. Store refrigerated in an airtight container for up to 1 week.

CREAMY DILL SAUCE

MAKES ABOUT 1¼ CUPS

2 small **scallions**, white and green parts, coarsely chopped (about ¼ cup)

½ cup loosely packed fresh **dill**, stems discarded

½ cup loosely packed **flat-leaf parsley** leaves

1 cup **mayonnaise**

3 tablespoons **sour cream**

5 teaspoons **white wine** or **white wine vinegar**

1 tablespoon **Dijon mustard**

¼ teaspoon **sea salt**, or more to taste

Freshly ground pepper to taste

Put the scallions, dill, and parsley in the bowl of a food processor and pulse several times until finely chopped and well combined. Add the mayonnaise, sour cream, wine, mustard, and salt and pepper to taste. Pulse 6 to 8 more times, or until the mixture is thoroughly combined and creamy. Use immediately or store refrigerated in an airtight container for up to 1 week.

QUICK MARINARA SAUCE

MAKES 2 CUPS

3 tablespoons **extra-virgin olive oil**

1 medium **Spanish onion**, finely chopped (about 1 cup)

3 medium **garlic cloves**, finely minced

2 cups **canned crushed tomatoes**

2 tablespoons **tomato paste**

10 fresh **basil** leaves, julienned (about ¼ cup)

¼ teaspoon dried **oregano**

Sea salt and **freshly ground pepper** to taste

Put the oil in a large sauté pan and heat over medium. Add the onions and sauté until softened, about 5 minutes. Add the garlic and cook for another 30 seconds. Add the crushed tomatoes, the tomato paste, and ¼ cup water and bring to a slow boil. Stir in the basil, oregano, and salt and pepper to taste, then lower the heat and simmer for another 20 minutes. Use immediately or store refrigerated in an airtight container for up to 1 week.

CLASSIC TARTAR SAUCE

MAKES A GENEROUS ½ CUP

3 tablespoons coarsely chopped **onion**

3 **cornichon**, coarsely chopped

1 tablespoon drained **capers**

½ cup **mayonnaise**

2 teaspoons freshly squeezed **lemon juice**

1 teaspoon **Dijon mustard**

1 teaspoon **distilled white vinegar**

½ teaspoon **Worcestershire sauce**

½ teaspoon **cornichon juice**

Freshly ground pepper to taste

1 tablespoon finely chopped **flat-leaf parsley**

Put the onion, cornichon, and capers in a food processor and pulse several times until finely minced, scraping down the sides of the bowl as needed. Add the mayonnaise, lemon juice, mustard, vinegar, Worcestershire, cornichon juice, and pepper to taste and pulse again until well combined. Scrape the sauce into a serving bowl and stir in the parsley. Use immediately or store refrigerated in an airtight container for up to 1 week.

THE
NEW
FULTON
FISH
MARKET

WE'RE A MAJOR PLAYER at the Fulton Fish Market in Hunts Point, NY. Over thirty years ago, I purchased the wholesale seafood company Lockwood & Winant to eliminate the middleman and offer the freshest seafood to our retail customers. The strength of direct relationships to fishermen allows us to offer a larger selection. We've maintained our now forty-year relationships with generations of wholesalers and fishermen who appreciate dependable partners in business. In 2007, we opened Meat Without Feet, a seafood supplier to leading restaurants, building a reputation with chefs for consistency and reliability.

HOW TO
PREP
FISH & SEAFOOD

By now you should know I encourage you to ask your fishmonger to do the work for you, but if you're ready to move on and try it yourself, here's how to prep a few seafood items. Go to citarella.com to watch me fillet a fish in action.

HOW TO SHUCK OYSTERS

1. Using an oyster knife (see page 249), insert the blade into the top part of the shell, near the hinge, inserting it about halfway.

2. Hold the oyster in your hand so the nook faces toward the tip of your pointer finger, then twist the knife.

3. Run the blade along the top of the shell, scraping it to release the meat. Separate the shells and serve the oyster as desired.

HOW TO SHUCK CLAMS

1. Hold the clam in the hand covered with a shucking glove or towel with the nook facing toward the tip of your pointer finger and the hinge facing toward the area of your palm near your thumb. With the other hand, slide the blade of a clam knife (see page 249) into the side of the shell.

2. Continue to slide the blade until you hit the hinge. Twist the knife down slightly, then run the blade along the top of the shell, scraping it to release the meat by loosening it, not cutting through it.

3. Slide the knife underneath the clam in the bottom shell as well. Pull off the top shell and serve the clam in the bottom shell or use as desired.

HOW TO FILLET A WHOLE GRILLED FISH

1. Place your knife blade in the center of the fish, and cut down with the tip of your knife until you touch the bone. Next, run a knife along the center of the fish, from the tail to the neck, then run it along the top, where the fin is.

2. Next slide the knife blade under the flesh, toward the spine and flat against the bones, and separate the flesh from the bones.

3. Lift out the piece of fish and set it aside.

4. Ride your knife along the bottom half of the center bone and release the piece of fish. Holding the tail, slide your knife under the bone, and run the blade along the underside of the fish skeleton, and pull it away from the flesh as you cut forward.

HOW TO DEVEIN SHRIMP

1. Peel the raw shrimp and discard the shells.

2. Run a deveiner tool or a knife along the back of the shrimp to expose the vein.

3. Gently remove the vein using the tip of the tool or knife, or your fingers. Rinse the deveined shrimp and refrigerate until ready to use.

HOW TO REMOVE COOKED LOBSTER MEAT

1. Put the cooked lobster on a cutting board and insert a knife in the middle of the back and pull the knife toward the tail. Turn the lobster around and insert the knife back in the middle and cut toward the top.

2. Pull the lobster apart and discard the sac and remove the meat.

3. To crack the claws, using the heel of the knife, hit down one time in the middle of the claw, only cutting about halfway through it. Then twist your knife, breaking the shell away from the claw meat.

4. Lastly wiggle the pincer claw from side to side and gently pull the claw apart. The meat should come out easily.

JOE'S

SEAFOOD
KITCHEN
ESSENTIALS

HANDLING AND STORING

Most fresh fish should be consumed within two days from the purchase date. Store the fish in the coldest part of your refrigerator, which is usually in the back near the freezer. Shellfish should be removed from the packaging and stored in a bowl in the refrigerator. Use within forty-eight hours.

I do not recommend freezing fish, but I know sometimes it's the best option if you've bought an expensive piece of fish and don't have time to cook it. To freeze, wrap the fish very well in plastic wrap. Put your package in a plastic freezer bag. Never use aluminum foil, as it's not airtight. Date and label your freezer packages. Masking tape and permanent marker hold up well. Freeze fish and seafood up to two months.

To defrost, put frozen fish, still in its packaging, in the refrigerator or under clean, cool running water. Do not refreeze defrosted fish.

RECOMMENDED PORTIONS

When you're buying fish, generally aim for ⅓ to ½ pound of meat per person. It's slightly more than you usually account for when buying chicken or beef. I've included a guide for general portion sizes. You may find they are larger than restaurant portions, which is because fish is light, and in my opinion not overly filling, so I like hearty portions. I leave it to you to determine what works for you—this is just a guide. You can always ask your fishmonger's advice as well. Depending on the number of sides, appetizers, and other accompaniments, your portion sizes may vary.

If you get one big fillet from your fishmonger, cut it into individual portions before cooking to ensure accurate cooking times. Plus, the smaller size is easier to move and handle with a spatula.

A lot of my recipes are written for four people, and there are some that serve two. You can easily double or triple quantities. I usually note in the recipes which ones work well for a crowd, like Stuffed Calamari (page 71), White Wine–Steamed Mussels (page 139), and Parmigiano-Dusted Baked Oysters (page 63). Generally, anything made on the stovetop is more difficult to prepare for larger numbers.

HANDY GUIDE TO
Fish & Seafood
PORTION SIZES

—

WHOLE FISH
¾ to 1 pound of raw fish
per person

FILLETS & STEAKS
6 to 8 ounces raw weight
per person

SEAFOOD
8 to 10 ounces raw weight
per person

COOKED MUSSELS & CLAMS
3 to 6 pieces as an
appetizer or 8 to 12 pieces
as a main course

RAW OYSTERS & CLAMS
6 pieces as an appetizer

SHRIMP
6 pieces as an appetizer or
12 pieces as a main course

JOE'S FAVORITE KITCHEN TOOLS

FISH OR PERFORATED SPATULA I prefer a large perforated turner (see Sources) because it's sturdy and the offset handle helps for better handling of fish.

RIMMED BAKING SHEET Indispensable for roasting and baking seafood; they hold up to broiling as well.

FRENCH GRILL Larger than most grill pans, this type of stovetop grill has a sloped design (see Sources).

A FEW POTS AND PANS Throughout the book, I refer to pots and sauté pans as small, medium, and large. Use these measurements as a general guide when choosing your cooking equipment:

Small Pot or Saucepan
about 1½ to 2 quarts

Medium Pot or Saucepan
4 to 6 quarts

Large Stock Pot
12 to 14 quarts

Medium Sauté Pan or Skillet
8 to 10 inches in diameter

Large Sauté Pan
12 inches or more

PARCHMENT PAPER This food-safe, disposable paper prevents foods from sticking to baking sheets—and best of all, it makes cleanup easy.

SHARP KNIVES A sharp knife is crucial when prepping raw fish, or most any ingredient for that matter. A well-cared-for knife will make your life much easier (and NEVER put a knife in the dishwasher).

CUTTING BOARDS ALWAYS use a wood or plastic cutting board. Cutting on marble or glass will dull your knife.

CLAM KNIFE A small knife with a rounded tip used to open clams by sliding the blade between the two shells.

OYSTER KNIFE A small knife with a narrow pointed blade that has tapered edges and is used to pry oyster shells open. It is shorter and squatter than a clam knife.

SHUCKING GLOVE A sturdy glove, sometimes made from steel mesh, that protects your hands when opening oysters and clams.

SOURCES

BRIDGE KITCHENWARE
bridgekitchenware.com

Online retailer for professional indoor French grills, skillets, and other kitchen tools.

CITARELLA GOURMET MARKET
citarella.com

Shop online, call 212-874-0383, or stop by any of the seven retail locations for pristine seafood and other high-quality food products. Fedex Priority Overnight shipping available everywhere in the US. Oyster and clam knives and shrimp deveiners available here too.

JB PRINCE
jbprince.com

Online retailer for professional culinary equipment and culinary tools, including Joe's favorite large perforated spatula.

WILLIAMS-SONOMA
williams-sonoma.com

Source for professional-quality cookware, including All-Clad pans, Global and Shun knives, and other cooking utensils.

ACKNOWLEDGMENTS

I have some really good, kind, strong people around me that have helped me along the course of my life, my career, and this book. Writing and putting together this book has been fun and a tremendous learning experience.

A huge thanks to my amazing wife, Yusi, the coolest mima on the planet, who I love even more than fish and whose opinion I respect more than anyone's; to my incredible assistant Nancy Palmarini, the most awesome loyal lady who does it all; to May Quon, my personal assistant; to my children Helen, Nancy, and Anthony, I love you and your spouses. My children's passion for this business makes me proud. To the Gonzalez and Valerio ladies, thank you for your love; to John Corbo and Anthony Bencivenga, who have been my right-hand men at Citarella and Lockwood & Winant respectively and dear friends for decades.

A big thanks also to my Citarella seafood people: Ralph Adames, Kevin Gomez, and Mike Rodriguez, because of them I was able to take on Lockwood in addition to Citarella. I'd also like to acknowledge Fedele Bruno, Charlie Gagliardo, Allen Greenberg (it has been a fun, crazy, long road—still so much to come), and the entire Citarella family.

I'd also like to extend my gratitude to Leo de St. Aubin, Adam Kolenberg, Chris Leary, Mike Leidner, Frankie Montalbano, Steve Rosso and the entire Lockwood & Winant family, and Pat Lohan and the Meat Without Feet family.

To Vinnie McCaffrey for selling me Citarella and Abe Haymes for selling me Lockwood & Winant.

Thanks also to my book team: Amy Collins, for orchestrating this tremendous project, talented photographer Bill Milne (your experience has been invaluable) and his assistant Noah Rosenbaum, my writing collaborator Rebecca Miller Ffrench (for your commitment and sense of humor and "getting me"), designer Laura Palese (you saw to it that we put out a beautiful book), editor Elinor Hutton, copyeditor Kathryn Wilson, publicist Carrie Bachman, writer Ann Callaghan, recipe tester Sandy Murzin, and food stylist Hadas Smirnoff and prop stylist Stephanie Hanes for their work on the cover.

Thank you to all my wonderful friends who let me work out my recipes on them and share great times around my kitchen island!

There are so many people who supported me, encouraged me and believed in my vision, and ran head on into new endeavors with me. I may have forgotten to print some names, but I have not forgotten you in my heart.

Food and family go hand in hand. Sitting with my grandboys and sharing a meal fills my heart. To my grandboys, Papi loves you! Thank you for adding so much joy to my life!

Lastly, to all my Citarella customers over the years—Thank You!

Top, left to right: The Gurrera Family—Yusi, Anthony, Helen, Joe, Nancy

INDEX

**BAY SCALLOPS
IN SHELL**

**WE WANT OUR READERS TO BE SAFE AND HEALTHY
WHEN CONSUMING FISH AND SHELLFISH.**

We'd like to direct you to the website www.fda.gov
for information relating specifically to seafood safety.
Please take the time to review this website for pertinent
information concerning the health and safety of
consuming fish. Generally speaking, consuming raw or
undercooked meats, poultry, seafood, shellfish, or eggs
may increase your risk of food borne illness, especially if
you have a medical condition.

JOE GURRERA is the owner of Citarella, a group of popular epicurean markets, which started with one of the original and most-respected neighborhood seafood shops in New York. Joe grew up in the fish business, learning firsthand the subtle differences between the flavors and textures of dozens of varieties of seafood. Joe also owns Lockwood & Winant, a wholesale company at the iconic Fulton Fish Market, and the hospitality seafood purveyor Meat Without Feet, which supplies some of the most prestigious restaurants in the United States. Joe is an industry leader selling several million pounds of seafood a year.